Christmas Carols

The Stories Behind the Songs

Tonya Lambert

BLUE
BIKE
BOOKS

First printed in 2012 10 9 8 7 6 5 4 3 2 1

Printed in Canada

The Publisher: Blue Bike Books

Website: www.bluebikebooks.com

Library and Archives Canada Cataloguing in Publication

Lambert, Tonya Marie

      Christmas carols : the stories behind the songs / Tonya Lambert.

ISBN 978-1-926700-39-7

      1. Carols--History and criticism. 2. Christmas music--

Miscellanea. I. Title.

ML2880.L222 2012   782.28'1723   C2012-904305-2

Project Director: Nicholle Carrière
Project Editor: Sheila Quinlan
Cover Image: photo of carolers in doorway: © Adrian Sherratt / Alamy;
lights around doorway: © Thinkstock
Illustrations: Roger Garcia, Peter Tyler, Roly Wood, Patrick Hénaff,
Amy Lambert

Produced with the assistance of the Government of Alberta, **Government**
Alberta Multimedia Development Fund. **of Alberta ∎**

We acknowledge the financial support of the Government of Canada
through the Canada Book Fund (CBF) for our publishing activities.

Canadian   Patrimoine
Heritage   canadien

PC: 1

DEDICATION

For my parents, Rudy and Eileen Lambert.
Thanks for everything.

ACKNOWLEDGMENTS

First and foremost, I would like to thank my dad, Rudy Lambert, for encouraging me in my writing from a very young age. He continues to support me today and with this project by searching for interesting bits of information and proofreading my work. Thanks also to my three daughters, Becky, Mary and Amy Lambert, for their interesting ideas for topics as well as their help in searching for information.

I would also like to acknowledge the support of four teachers, who encouraged my writing by providing me with time and feedback. Joan Gowda (grade one) and Brenda Peniuk (grade three) taught me at Kelvington Elementary School. Judy Patenaude (grade eight) and Candace Patrick (grades 10 and 11) were my English teachers at Kelvington High School.

Finally, thanks to Nicholle Carriére and my editor Sheila Quinlan for all their help in making this book a reality. Thanks, Nicholle, for suggesting the subject of Christmas carols in the first place.

CONTENTS

I pray you, sirs, both more and less,
Sing these carols in Christëmas.

–John Awdlay, chaplain of Haughmond Abbey,
Shropshire (c. 1426)

INTRODUCTION

The songs of Christmas are many and varied, some very old and some brand new. The most popular and successful are those that have been able to create a feeling of belonging. Christmas carols seek to unite all humankind. Indeed, the feeling of unity in carols extends even beyond people to embrace all living creatures.

Christmas music unites the past with the present. Just imagine, some of the carols that we sing every year are the same ones that were sung by our ancestors hundreds of years ago. Even traces of the pre-Christian past of our forebears can be found in some carols, the songs revealing the Christianization of folk customs and the folklorization of Christianity.

By adopting a time of festive celebration for many pre-Christian religions (December 25 is only a few days removed from the Winter Solstice), the celebration of Christmas has always been a curious blend of the pagan, Christian and secular. Indeed, throughout history different groups of people have placed the emphasis of their own holiday festivities on various aspects of the occasion—some favoring the Christian celebration of the birth of Jesus, others focusing on the secular activities of feasting, drinking, partying and gift-giving originally contrived to get people through the darkest and coldest part of the year. Not surprisingly, there are songs that celebrate both of these preferences. However, even though Christmas has sometimes been a contest between Christian solemnity and secular merry-making, the holiday has more often been a happy mixture of both.

Carols evoke a wide range of emotions. There are songs of deep reverence for the mystery of Christ's birth. There are songs of joy, celebrating the promise of humanity's redemption from sin as well as the reuniting of family and friends during the holiday season. There are sad songs about people unable to be with loved ones at Christmas or about people who do not have the financial means to celebrate in the commercialized way popular today. There are even humorous songs, designed to make people laugh and forget about the cares and stresses of daily life.

This book explores many of the songs of Christmas, looking at the stories behind their creation and their uses throughout the years. It looks at the wide variety of cultural traditions surrounding the singing of these songs, both past and present. However, I make no claim to having included every song of the season. There are simply too many. Nonetheless, I hope that you do find some interesting new information in these pages and that I have provided you with a bit of holiday entertainment. Finally, I would like to leave you with a Christmas wish in the words of carolers in Skipton, England, two hundred years ago:

I wish you a merry Christmas,
And a happy New Year–
A pocketful of money,
And a barrelful of beer!

Carol: The Word

🔔 The word "carol" originally meant a song that was danced in a ring. It was in no way unique to Christmas and has its roots in ancient Greece. *Choros* was the ancient Greek word for a circle dance.

🔔 In Latin, the term *choraula* referred to a dance accompanied by a reed instrument, such as a flute.

🔔 A 7th-century edict from Rouen forbade people to participate in *caraulas* (dance-songs).

🔔 In 12th-century France, *carole* was a term used by troubadours and referred to a flirtatious song and dance typically associated with May Day celebrations.

🔔 Chaucer provides one of the earliest uses of the word "carol" in the English language. In his 14th-century poem "The Romance of the Rose," he refers to dancing as caroling: "daunceth with us now, / And I, without tarying, / Wente into the caroling."

🔔 By the 15th century, the term "carol" was being applied to songs sung (and likely danced) during the Christmas season.

🔔 A carol originally applied to a dance song with a strict form, one which alternated between verses and a repeated refrain. Generally, the verses were sung by one person with everyone else joining in on the refrain. Such a definition would rule out many songs today referred to as Christmas carols.

🔔 The old Polish word for Christmas carols was *symfonia* (symphony). The modern Polish word for "carol"—*kolęda*—is also the word for "gift." The songs of carolers are their gift to the household, which reciprocates with gifts of treats or money.

🔔 The Romanian *colinde* and Bulgarian *koledari* also mean both "carol" and "gift."

The German word for Christmas songs is *Weihnachtslieder*, meaning "white night songs."

 In Italian, the term *canzoni di Natale*, meaning "songs of the Nativity," refers to religious songs sung at Christmas.

THE START OF SINGING TO THE REFORMATION

Early Christian Nativity Chants

There was very little music in the early church because the use of music in religious worship was connected by the early followers of Christ to the practices of the Judaic religion. However, there was a form of bare-bones music performed by the clergy in the form of a chant. This was originally done *a capella*—that is, without any instrumental accompaniment.

Three very early Christian hymns dealing with Christ's birth are Ambrose's (died 397) "Come, Redeemer of the Peoples" (*Veni, Redemptor Gentium*), which was written in opposition to Arianism; Aurelius Clemens Prudentius' (c. 348–407) "Of the Father's Love Begotten" (*Corde Natus ex Parentis*); and Coelius Sedulius' (died c. 450) "From the Lands that See the Sun Arise" (*A Solis Ortus Cardine*). Sedulius' work is still sung in Roman Catholic churches on Christmas Day. These early Latin hymn chants were all focused on the theology of the church rather than on the more narrative aspects of the religion.

Of the Father's Love Begotten

Prudentius' early chant *Corde Natus ex Parentis* was translated into English by John Mason Neale in 1851. Roby Furley Davis, dissatisfied with Neale's translation, wrote a different version in 1906. Neale's translation is entitled "Of the Father's Love Begotten" while Davis' is called "Of the Father's Heart Begotten."

Prudentius' chant first appeared in his *Liber Cathemerinon* as hymn nine. The lyrics were paired with a plainsong known as *Divinum Mysterium* ("Divine Mystery") very early on, and several manuscripts from the 10th to the 16th centuries have survived. The first print version is found in the 1582 Finnish collection of songs called *Piae Cantiones* ("Devout Songs").

DID YOU KNOW?

The first recorded use of the term Christmas, or Christ's mass, dates from 1038.

The Development of Carol Singing

St. Bernard of Clairvaux
One aspect of the Christmas service in the Roman Catholic Church is the singing of the *Laetabundus, exsultet fidelis* ("Come rejoicing, faithful men, with rapture singing"). It was written in the early 12th century by St. Bernard of Clairvaux (1090–1153).

St. Bernard of Clairvaux was a member of a religious order called the Cistercians. The order had been founded not long after Bernard's birth and he himself was highly instrumental in its rapid spread across Europe. The Cistercians combined the life of a monk with that of a farm laborer.

St. Bernard was a religious reformer. He founded the Cistercian abbey at Clairvaux, where he was abbot. He was very influential in the church, aiding in the ending of a papal schism (1130–1138) and co-organizing the Second Crusade (1145–1149).

St. Bernard's *Laetabundus, exsultet fidelis* spread widely throughout Europe, becoming especially popular in England and France. It was unique in that the stanzas rhymed. This notion of rhyming stanzas was soon adopted by many other writers of verse.

St. Francis of Assisi
St. Francis of Assisi (born Giovanni Francesco di Bernardone, date uncertain) grew up in a well-to-do family; his father was

a cloth merchant. As a young man, St. Francis was high-spirited and adventurous, enjoying a good party and the life of a soldier. He particularly enjoyed the troubadours and their songs. Then, after having a vision, he chose to leave all that behind and devote his life to God and the Church. He received permission from the pope for he and his followers to live as preachers. They were known as Franciscans. Their goal was to make religion more accessible to the average person.

In 1223, St. Francis was in the Italian town of Grecio at Christmas. The local church was too small to hold the number of people who came to hear him preach, so St. Francis set up an altar outside of town. He then assembled some animals and created a manger scene. This was the first time such a thing had been done. He also encouraged the people to join in the singing in their native tongue, another first.

Both the practice of setting up a manger scene and the singing of religious songs in the vernacular quickly caught on and spread across the Mediterranean world. St. Francis lived for only three more years after that Christmas service at Grecio, dying in 1226. His feast day in the Roman Catholic Church is October 4.

Jacopone da Todi

Jacopone da Todi (1228–1306) was a lay member of the Franciscan Order who suffered greatly for his beliefs. He had been born into a noble family, married and became a lawyer. His life changed when his wife died in a freak accident; the floor on which she was dancing collapsed beneath her. When da Todi saw that his wife had been wearing a haircloth under her fine clothes, he was greatly affected. (A haircloth was a coarse piece of woollen cloth worn next to the skin. It irritated the skin and was meant to be a constant reminder of one's sins.)

Jacopone quit his legal practice and joined the Franciscans. The young order was by then split into two factions, and Jacopone joined the group that followed the more severely ascetic life. When Boniface VIII became pope in 1298, he tried to force the members of Jacopone's group to join the others. Some, including Jacopone, refused. As a result, Jacopone was excommunicated and imprisoned in a dungeon for the next five years. After his release he retired to Collazzone, where he died three years later during Midnight Mass on Christmas Eve.

Jacopone da Todi wrote many religious poems and songs, a number of them on the topic of Jesus' birth. His lyrics were realistic in nature, making them accessible to both the educated and the illiterate alike, and they were spread throughout Europe by traveling Franciscan preachers. He was the first writer to compose a large number of hymns and poems celebrating the Nativity. He wrote both the *Stabat Mater Dolorosa* ("Sorrows of Mary") and the *Stabat Mater Speciosa* ("Joys of Mary"). The latter concerns the birth of Jesus and has provided the inspiration for several Christmas songs and instrumental pieces. The Polish composer Paul Bebenek set *Stabat Mater Speciosa* to music, translating the lyrics into Polish. Another Christmas song, "The Beautiful Mother," is a translation of a poem by Jacopone.

The Song of the Sibyl

Since time immemorial, there have been people who have claimed to be able to see the future. To the people of ancient Greece, such people were known as sibyls and they were always female. People would travel long distances to ask a question of the most famous sibyl, the one at Delphi. During the Middle Ages, after the fall of Rome and the rise of Christianity, the ancient sibyls were adopted by the church as prophets of the Apocalypse.

On the Spanish island of Majorca in the Mediterranean Sea and the Italian island of Sardinia nearby, a curious song has survived from the medieval period. It is known as "The Song of the Sibyl," and it is sung at Midnight Mass on Christmas Eve by a young soloist. The song was originally a Gregorian chant sung in Latin. However, by the 13th century, the lyrics had been translated into the local Catalan language in which they are still sung today. The Catalan lyrics were translated from the French Provençal, into which the song had been first translated from the Latin.

"The Song of the Sibyl" was once much more widespread than it is today. The Council of Trent, which was held by the Roman Catholic Church between 1545 and 1563 to reform and universalize the teachings and practices of the Church, banned the performance of "The Song of the Sibyl" (known then as "Book of the Final Judgment"), once an integral part of the liturgy. Helped along into obscurity by the spread of Protestantism, the song died out everywhere but on Majorca and Sardinia. But having survived this long, it is not likely to disappear now— UNESCO (United Nations Educational, Scientific and Cultural Organization) declared it a Masterpiece of the Oral and Intangible Heritage of Humanity on November 16, 2010.

While the sibyl in the song is a woman, the singer of the song is usually a boy because it was frowned upon for women to sing in church for many centuries. The singer carries a sword that is held aloft during the song and is used to make the sign of the cross afterward.

Early Anglo-Norman Secular Celebrations

The earliest known Christmas carol in England is in the Anglo-Norman dialect of the 12th century and contains no religious references. It is basically a drinking song with lines such as "Lordings, Christmas loves good drinking."

This carol gives us some idea of how Christmas was kept in medieval England. Lords were expected to keep an open house where all their tenants were welcome to come to their hall and partake of food and drink and the warmth of a roaring fire. Celebrations lasted for 12 days, during which time a large log called the Yule log burned in the hearth. It was a time for merriment and relaxation; few people were expected to work (except the poor cooks, who were kept very busy). Entertainment was provided by traveling minstrels as well as by the guests themselves.

This song is an example of the secular celebrations related to the season, celebrations that long pre-date the birth of Jesus and the Christian celebration of that event. These festivities had their roots in centuries of Winter Solstice celebrations, designed to keep away the evil spirits on the longest night of the year as well as to celebrate the increasing length of the day henceforth. In agricultural societies, there is little to do during the long, cold winter months, aside from care for the few animals that each family possessed, so the time was passed in various ways including visiting with neighbors and singing.

That early Christmas songs and celebrations were secular in nature with the Christian component being a later addition can be seen in more than a few surviving lyrics. A 1497 biographer of Thomas à Becket was of the opinion that Christmas carols were a bad influence on the young, so many of them must have been of a bawdy nature espousing drinking, feasting and other forms of merry-making.

DID YOU  KNOW?

The earliest known Christmas carol in the English language is "A Child is Boren Amonges Men." It was written in a set of sermon notes by a Franciscan friar in the early 14th century.

"Wait"-ing for a Merry Christmas
Singers and musicians who walked around singing and playing Christmas music at night were known as "waits" in England. The first wait, or minstrel, was hired by Edward III (r. 1327–1377). By the early 16th century, waits were performing the joint tasks of caroling and being night watchmen. Each wait had a reed instrument with which to signal the passing of the hours.

The carols "God Rest Ye Merry, Gentlemen" and "We Wish You a Merry Christmas" were sung by medieval waits. After singing their wishes for a good Christmas and a prosperous new year, the waits would often receive some sort of thanks, such as figgy pudding, in return. "We Wish You a Merry Christmas" originated in western England. "God Rest Ye Merry, Gentlemen" is an old carol of unknown origin. The tune dates back to at least 1580, when it accompanied a ballad about the London earthquake.

Today, the word "merry" means "happy," but when the carol "God Rest Ye Merry, Gentlemen" was written, it meant "great" or "mighty" (e.g., Robin Hood and his Merry Men). The word "rest" also had a different meaning, that of "keep" or "make." Thus, in modern English, "God rest ye merry, gentlemen" translates as "God make you mighty, gentlemen"; it is a blessing. When one says "Merry Christmas," what they are saying is, "Have a great Christmas."

Both carols are still popular today. "God Rest Ye Merry, Gentlemen" is the song that the hungry child stops to sing outside Ebenezer Scrooge's counting house on Christmas Eve in Charles Dickens' *A Christmas Carol* before Scrooge chases him away with a ruler. "We Wish You a Merry Christmas" has appeared in several recent films: *Precious* (2009), *The Santa Clause 3: The Escape Clause* (2006), *College Road Trip* (2008), *Crash* (2004), *Disaster Movie* (2008), *Mothman Prophecies* (2002), *National Lampoon's Dorm Daze* (2003), *Reindeer Games* (2000), *Rent-a-Cop* (1987) and *Sleepless in Seattle* (1993).

DID YOU KNOW?

In 1991, the phrase "Merry Christmas" was banned by town councillors in Newtown, Wales, from being publicly displayed. The councillors felt that the word "merry" could mean drunkenness, a condition they did not want to encourage during the holiday season. It was decided that the phrase "Happy Christmas" would be used instead.

The Coventry Carol

Coventry is a city in the West Midlands of England. During the Middle Ages, Coventry, like many other cities in England and Europe, adopted the practice of holding a series of Biblical plays put on by the various trade guilds in celebration of Corpus Christi. The Feast of Corpus Christi celebrates the presence of the body and blood of Christ in the Eucharist and only came into being in the second half of the 13th century. However, it quickly caught on and became very popular. Like Easter, the date of the feast changed every year, being the third Thursday after Trinity Sunday (somewhere between May 21 and June 24).

In Coventry, the Corpus Christi Mystery Plays are first recorded as being presented in 1393, and they continued to be performed every year until they were suppressed by the Reformation in 1579. The oldest known text was written down by Robert Croo in 1534, and the first published version dates from 1591. There were at least 10 plays in the cycle, of which only two still survive: *The Pageant of the Shearmen and the Tailors*, portraying the events from the Annunciation of Mary to the Murder of the Holy Innocents, and *The Pageant of the Weavers*, enacting the tale of Jesus' life from the Purification to the scene with the doctors in the temple. The plays were attended by members from every station of society, including royalty. Queen Margaret, wife of Henry VI, as well as King Richard III, King Henry VII, King Henry VIII and Queen Elizabeth I are known to have witnessed the plays in 1456, 1484, 1492, 1511 and 1566, respectively.

The song "Lullay, Thou Little Tiny Child" is from *The Pageant of the Shearmen and the Tailors*. In the play, it was sung by the women of Bethlehem to their infant sons just before Herod's soldiers arrived to kill the boys. It is the grieving lament of a helpless mother. In the years since the suppression of the Mystery Plays, "Lullay, Thou Little Tiny Child" has become associated with the Christmas season. Its origins have led to it being widely known as "The Coventry Carol." The song is quite well known in Britain and has been recorded by many modern singers, including Tori Amos, Joan Baez, Annie Lennox and Loreena McKennitt.

DID YOU  KNOW?

The German Christmas carol "Song of the Crib" was also originally part of a Mystery Play. The earliest extant version dates from the 15th century and is in Leipzig University.

The Cherry Tree Carol

Like "The Coventry Carol," "The Cherry Tree Carol" is thought to be a survival from a Corpus Christi Mystery Play. It is quite likely that it is from one of the missing cycles of the most famous of these plays, the ones presented at Coventry.

"The Cherry Tree Carol" is based on the apocryphal story in chapter 20 of the Pseudo-Matthew Gospel (one of the gospels not chosen to be part of the New Testament). The tree in that story is a date tree. The story was well known throughout Europe in the Middle Ages. In Spain and France, the fruit tree is an apple tree.

Because the song is so old and survived for centuries only as part of the oral tradition, three distinct versions sung to a wide variety of tunes have made it to the present day in areas of both England and North America. All the songs begin with the same story. As a pregnant Mary and her husband Joseph journey to be taxed, they pass a cherry orchard. Mary is hungry and asks Joseph to pick some cherries for her and the baby. Joseph retorts that the baby's father can get her some cherries. In one version, God makes the tree branches bend so Mary can reach some cherries. In another version, an angel appears to Joseph and explains the circumstances surrounding his wife's pregnancy. In the third version, Jesus is a small child sitting in his mother's lap telling her about what his future life on earth holds for him.

"The Cherry Tree Carol" has been recorded numerous times and in several languages besides English, such as Italian, French and Spanish. Joan Baez, Sting and EmmyLou Harris, as well as Peter, Paul and Mary, are all well-known performers who have recorded the song. All the above-mentioned sing the lyrics where the tree bends down so Mary can reach some cherries.

The Seven Joys of Mary

"The Seven Joys of Mary" is a very old Christmas song, dating to at least the 14th century, that was undoubtedly inspired by the popular medieval rosary devotion on the Seven Joys of Mary: 1) the Annunciation; 2) the Nativity; 3) the Adoration of the Magi; 4) the Resurrection of Christ; 5) the Ascension of Christ into Heaven; 6) the Pentecost; and 7) the Coronation of Mary in Heaven. This carol is another one likely performed in the popular Mystery Plays of the Middle Ages.

The Seven Joys of Mary listed in the song are very different, with the English and American versions varying somewhat. In England, the joys that Mary received from her son Jesus are his suckling at her breast, his curing the lame, his curing the blind, his raising the dead, his carrying the cross, his wearing the Crown of Heaven and his writing with a golden pen. In the American version, the joys Jesus provided Mary with are his being born, his curing the lame, his curing the blind, his reading in the temple, his raising the dead, his rising from the dead and his wearing the Crown of Heaven.

The differences in the English and American versions are largely the result of the religious beliefs of their earliest singers. The song, with its strong Catholic bent, clearly pre-dates the Reformation in England. However, the Protestant settlers in America changed the lyrics to reflect their beliefs—for example, the emphasis on Jesus reading the Old Testament in the temple.

Protestantism is far more centered upon the Bible and the ability of the laity to read it than is Catholicism, with its rituals, traditions and saints' lives.

🔔 "The Seven Joys of Mary," like "The Twelve Days of Christmas" (see p. 47), is one of many numeral songs dating from the days when few people were literate. People had to rely upon their memories. Numeral verses were a popular learning tool. Children who remembered all the verses (or the most verses) would be praised and rewarded.

🔔 In England, it used to be considered bad luck if the vessel maids (see p. 37) did not come to your door before Christmas Eve to sing "The Seven Joys of Mary."

🔔 Burl Ives and Great Big Sea are two modern artists who have recorded the song.

Good Christian Men, Rejoice

"Good Christian Men, Rejoice" is the English name for the German and Latin carol *In Dulci Jubilo* ("In Sweet Jubilation"). In his autobiography *The Little Book of Eternal Wisdom*, written in 1328, the German mystic and Dominican monk Heinrich Suso (1295–1366) claims to have written the lyrics and music for *In Dulci Jubilo* after being inspired by a dream in which angels danced and sang the song.

🔔 *In Dulci Jubilo* was written in a combination of German and Latin. A song written in more than one language is referred to as macaronic.

🔔 The oldest known manuscript of *In Dulci Jubilo* is in Leipzig University (codex 1305). It dates from c. 1400 and is a single-verse dance song.

🔔 Three more verses were added anonymously during the 15th century.

🔔 The first printed version of this song appeared in a Lutheran hymn book of 1533 compiled by Joseph Klug. It included three of the four known verses. The excluded verse was considered to be too Catholic for inclusion.

🔔 By 1582, a Swedish/Latin version of this carol existed.

🔔 Robert Lucas de Pearsall did an English/Latin translation of the carol in 1833. It is frequently sung as part of the Festival of Nine Lessons and Carols (see p. 193).

🔔 John Mason Neale wrote the best-known all-English version of the carol—"Good Christian Men, Rejoice."

O Come, O Come, Emmanuel

"O Come, O Come, Emmanuel" was originally a Gregorian chant or plainsong dating from at least the 9th century. It was sung *a cappella*. The tune to which "O Come, O Come, Emmanuel" is usually sung today first appeared in a 15th-century processional used by Franciscan nuns in France. The lyrics, translated by John Mason Neale, appeared in *Psalteriolum Cantionum Catholicarum* (Cologne, 1710).

"O Come, O Come, Emmanuel" is often a processional hymn in Roman Catholic churches on Sundays in Advent. The seven antiphons of which it is comprised are sung at vespers, one on each of the seven evenings prior to Christmas Eve. The seven "Great O's" are:

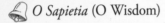 *O Sapietia* (O Wisdom)

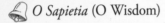 *O Adonai* (O Lord)

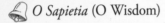 *O Radix Jesse* (O Root of Jesse)

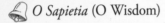 *O Clavis David* (O Key of David)

 O Oriens (O Day-Spring)

 O Rex (O King)

 O Emmanuel

Combining the first letter of each of the second words makes the acrostic SARCORE, which when read backward is *Ero cras*, meaning "I will be present tomorrow." This meaning is particularly apt for a series of antiphons sung on the Sundays leading up to Christmas. Medieval people loved riddles, and acrostics were popular with scholars of the period.

The First Nowell

The origin of "The First Nowell" is unknown, but it is thought to date back many centuries. It has the attributes of a folk song, including a genuine devotion coupled with a lack of Biblical accuracy (reflecting the inability of most medieval people to read). In the song, the shepherds see the Star of Bethlehem, an event that is not recorded in the Bible; in the Bible, it is the Wise Men who follow the star to Bethlehem.

Also, "The First Nowell," as recorded in the early 19th century, referred to three shepherds. The number of shepherds who received the angels' message of Christ's birth is not given in the Bible. However, three was the usual number of shepherds in medieval Mystery Plays and hints at the carol's long roots. The lyrics have since been altered, and today people sing, "to *certain* poor shepherds…"

"The First Nowell" is still a well-known and popular Christmas carol today. It has been recorded by many famous singers, including Carrie Underwood, Elvis Presley, Annie Lennox, Susan Boyle, Bob Dylan and Jackie Evancho.

DID YOU KNOW?

In the Chester Mystery Plays, the shepherds were named Harvey, Tudd and Trowle, while in some medieval legends four shepherds are named: Misael, Achael, Cyricus and Stephanus. Their names, along with those of the three Wise Men, were invoked in charms to cure snake bites.

The Shepherds' Story in Song

🔔 More Christmas carols are based on the shepherds' story than on that of the Wise Men.

🔔 A popular variety of Christmas song in German areas was the *Hirtenlieder*, or "shepherd songs." In these, the peasant singers closely identified with the shepherds who witnessed Jesus' birth.

🔔 The shepherds' visit to see the baby Jesus is a common theme of Polish religious carols.

Provençal shepherds used to sing in the fields on Christmas Eve in reminiscence of the shepherds on the fields near Bethlehem on the evening of Jesus' birth.

 "As Lately We Watched" is a traditional Christmas carol from Austria. It tells the story of Jesus' birth from the viewpoint of the shepherds.

More Medieval Melodies

Let the Voice of Praise Resound

"Let the Voice of Praise Resound" (*Resonet in Laudibus*) is another popular medieval Christmas hymn that has stood the test of time. Many copies of the text survive in both manuscript and print forms, the earliest being in the *Moosburg Gradual of 1360*. Writing in 1550, Georg Wicel called this hymn "one of the chief Christmas songs of joy." After the Reformation of the 16th century, it remained popular in both the Catholic and Lutheran churches.

The Blessed Virgin's Lullaby

"The Blessed Virgin's Lullaby" (*Angelus ad Virginum*) was a popular medieval Advent hymn. It was sung in Latin throughout Europe. Geoffrey Chaucer (1342–1400) referred to it in *The Miller's Tale*, where it is sung by Nicholas, the clerk of Oxenford. John Awdlay (died c. 1426) recorded part of it in his collection of carols. Earlier manuscript copies survive in Dublin and in Addle, in Yorkshire. It was reportedly 27 verses long originally, but only five verses have survived to the present day. It has since been set to the tune of the 16th-century dance song "Sellenger's Round."

Carol of the Beasts

"Carol of the Beasts" is a medieval French carol dating back to at least the 13th century. It was translated into English in the 1920s by Robert Davis (1881–1950). It is set to a Latin melody called *Orientis Partibus*. The song lists the gifts given by the various animals—cow, donkey, camel, sheep and dove—thought by medieval folks to have been present at the birth of Jesus. The carol is also known as "The Gifts of the Animals," "The Donkey Carol," "The Animal Carol" and "The Song of the Ass."

Burl Ives recorded "Carol of the Beasts" in 1952. Since then, several other artists have released their own versions. Harry Belafonte and Johnny Cash titled the piece "The Gifts They Gave."

DID YOU KNOW?

People in pre-industrial Europe believed that at midnight on Christmas Eve, the cattle and sheep knelt down, the eldest gander cried out and the hounds refused to chase the fox, all in honor of the birth of Our Lord.

Lullabies for Jesus

Lullabies are a very old genre of Christmas song, dating back to the medieval period. They are found in most European cultures.

Cradle-rocking carols, known as *Kindelwiegen* in German (i.e., "rocking of the child") were common from the 14th to the 16th centuries, originating in Germany and Austria. At first, the cradle holding the baby Jesus was rocked by two priests dressed as Mary and Joseph. The entire congregation sang carols like lullabies. Eventually, lay people also had a chance to rock the cradle.

Examples of cradle songs are *Lulajze Jezuniu* ("Slumber Little Jesus") from Poland, *Najej, Nynjej* ("Rocking") from the Czech Republic and *Quem Pastores Laudavere* ("Whom of Old the Shepherds Praised") from Germany.

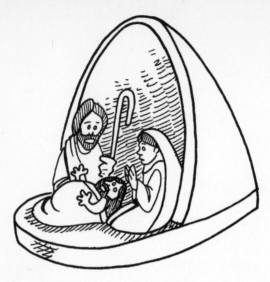

In some areas of Germany, it was customary to place a swaddled effigy of the baby Jesus on the altar after the Christmas mass. The children would dance around the altar and sing carols, probably lullabies. In Brixen, "rocking" used to be done every evening between Christmas and Candlemas by the sacristan. At Tübingen, a cradle was rocked on the tower of the main church at midnight on Christmas Eve while below people sang a cradle song. This tradition continued until 1830.

DID YOU  KNOW?

The Church of Santa Maria Maggiore in Rome claims to possess five pieces of wood from the manger that held the baby Jesus. It was brought to Rome from Bethlehem in the 7th century. Every Christmas Eve, these relics are placed on the High Altar for everyone to see.

Q: What's the favorite Christmas carol of new parents?

A: "Silent Night."

Early French Christmas Carols

Singing Christmas carols is known to have been a popular French custom by the 14th century. The Provençal carol "March of the Kings" (*La Marche des Rois*) dates back to at least the 13th century. The French province of Poitou is the main source for early French Christmas carols, with a number of them dating back to the 15th century. All the earlier carols of which we know were secular in nature. Popular secular Christmas songs in 15th- and 16th-century France were "The New Noël" (*Noël nouvelet*) and "William, Take Up Your Tambourine" (*Guillaume, prends ton tambourin*).

We know of several early writers of Christmas songs in France. The Catholic curé Lucas le Moigne published his *New Noël Songs (Chansons de Noëls Nouvaulx)* in 1520 while Mathieu Malingre (died 1572) edited a booklet of 24 Huguenot Christmas carols in 1533. Françoise Paschal of Lyons (born c. 1610) wrote carols in Latin. Two other early-modern French carol composers are known: Jean Daniel, a priest-organist at Nantes, and Nicholas Denisot (1515–1559) of Le Mans.

French carols are full of heartfelt devotion but little theological accuracy. Many songs place the singer in the position of being present at the birth of Jesus. The carols of both Nicholas Saboly (1614–1675) and Bernard de la Monnoye (1641–1728), while very different in many respects—Provençal Saboly's carols are kind and tender while Burgundian de la Monnoye's are witty and sarcastic—make the songs and Christ's birth very real and very personal for both the singer and the audience.

Bring a Torch, Jeanette, Isabella

The carol "Bring a Torch, Jeanette, Isabella" encapsulates the celebration of Christmas in the Provence region of southern France. There, as in many areas of southern Europe, the manger scene takes the place of a Christmas tree in the family home. Family members gather around the manger to sing songs and say prayers on Christmas Eve. The entire scene is lit by torchlight.

Making the manger was the job of the children of the household, who gathered sticks and moss and other materials to make it. The scene contained not only the characters mentioned in the Bible but representations of local people as well. The songs sung about the birth of Jesus also came to include references to local people. One wonders who were the Jeanette and Isabella referred to in this carol.

🔔 "Bring a Torch, Jeanette, Isabella" was first published in France in 1553.

🔔 The most well-known English version is by Edward Cuthbert Nunn (1868–1914).

🔔 In 1965, Smokey Robinson recorded "Bring a Torch, Jeanette, Isabella."

DID YOU KNOW?

French explorer Jacques Cartier (1491–1557) led his second expedition to North America in 1535. While wintering in Canada, his crew celebrated Christmas in what is now Quebec. They are recorded as having sung the French carol "Shepherds, Let Us Gather Here" (*Ça, Bergers, Assemblons Nous*) on Christmas Day.

Wassailing: A Christmas Tradition

Wassail, wassail, wassail, sing we,
In worship of Christ's Nativity
(pre-1536)

Wassailing is an English Christmas tradition that dates back to at least the 15th century and possibly earlier. In medieval England, drinking toasts were "Wassail!" meaning "Your health," followed by the reply "Drinkhail!" meaning "Drink health."

The Christmas banquets at the court of King Henry VIII included a huge wassail bowl. In the brew floated 12 crabapples to represent the twelve days of Christmas. Each crabapple had three cloves in it symbolizing the Holy Trinity.

In his 1622 poem "A Christmas Carol," English poet George Wither described the holiday festivities of the time. Included is a reference to the custom of women going door to door singing carols, carrying wassail bowls with them. These women were known as "wassail wenches" or "wassail virgins." After serenading the inhabitants, the wassailers would offer them a drink from their wassail bowl in return for a small token of appreciation.

Nicholas Culpepper's 1653 *Complete Herbal* contained a recipe for making Christmas wassail. The list of ingredients was as follows:

 two cinnamon sticks

 four cloves

 two blades of mace

 one ginger root

 four apples

 one teaspoonful of nutmeg

 four ounces of sugar

 half a pint of brown ale and cider

The Victorian author Charles Dickens, who was largely responsible for the revival of Christmas celebrations in the English-speaking world, wrote about the "mighty bowl of wassail in which the hot apples hissed and bubbled" (*The Pickwick Papers*, 1837). Sir Walter Scott described these bowls as being decorated with ribbon.

Luther's Carols

Martin Luther (1483–1546) was a German monk, priest and theologian whose attempts to reform the Catholic Church led to the Protestant Reformation. Lutheranism is the form of Christianity founded by Luther. He was a strong proponent of Christmas and celebrating the birth of Christ, unlike some other reformers. He encouraged the singing of hymns in praise of Jesus' birth and wrote five such songs himself. Indeed, in his Christmas sermon in 1542, Luther exhorted his young parishioners to "sing, dear children, sing about the newborn child! For if we do not sing about Him, about whom will we sing?"

The first Christmas hymn written by Luther is the best-known, "From Heaven Above to Earth I Come" (*Vom Himmel Hoch*), in 1535. He is said to have written it while rocking his daughter to sleep. The first verse is of medieval origin but Luther added the six other verses. He originally set the hymn to a popular tavern riddle song in the hopes that the new godly words would replace the old. However, such was not the case. The words were set to their present tune in 1551 by Johann Walther.

Luther's second carol, "Herod, Why Dreadest Thou a Foe," is actually a translation of an earlier Latin hymn. Luther wrote "From Heaven the Angel Troop Came Near" in 1543.

From Heaven Above to Earth I Come
There used to be an age-old custom in the town of Crimmitschau in Saxony whereby a boy, dressed as an angel, was lowered from

the roof of the church while singing Luther's hymn "From Heaven Above to Earth I Come." The practice was discontinued after the rope broke on one occasion in the 19th century, seriously injuring the young singer.

In the village of Oberufer in Hungary, a centuries-old series of plays is still performed during the Advent season. On the first Sunday in Advent, a procession is made to the hall led by a man carrying a star lantern (the Star Singer) and another with a small Christmas tree. The actors sing hymns, including "From Heaven Above to Earth I Come." The star, representing Jerusalem, is placed on stage when scenes are set in that city; the Christmas tree is placed on stage when scenes are in Bethlehem.

DID YOU  KNOW?

In the town of Weissenhorn, Germany, in 1524, people opposed to the religious celebration of Christmas disrupted church services on Christmas Day by singing satirical parodies of the holiday hymns.

England: Caroling Before the Commonwealth

When the Puritans came to power in England following the Civil War and the execution of King Charles I in 1649, they purged the country of many of its festive occasions, including Christmas. Before this time, and particularly before the religious turmoil of the middle of the 16th century, the English had been a people with many celebratory customs for the Christmas season. Caroling was extremely popular—at the royal court and in the churches, streets and houses of the nation. Holiday singing is mentioned by a number of the period's writers.

The earliest collection of Christmas carols is found in a manuscript compiled by John Awdlay (died c. 1426), a blind priest and poet of Haughmond Abbey in Shropshire.

In 1487 at King Henry VII's Christmas feast following Midnight Mass, the dean and choristers of the king's chapel were asked to sing a carol after the first course.

London's St. Mary-at-Hill churchwardens' accounts for 1537 include a notation for the payment made to a man for producing five copies of carol books for the church.

The Puritan influence can be seen in the 1550 booklet *Christmas Carols Newly Imprinted* by Richard Kele.

Thomas Tusser (1524–1580), in his *Five Hundred Pointes of Good Husbandrie* (1557), noted the singing of "jolie carols" as a holiday custom.

Describing an Elizabethan Christmas, contemporary Nicholas Breton (1545–1626) wrote, "It is now Christmas, and not a cup of drink must pass without a carol."

Thomas Kirchmeier, a Dutchman, wrote of his travels in England in his *Fourth Book of the Papal Kingdom* (1570). He noted that after Midnight Mass, the English placed a wooden figure of the baby Jesus on top of the altar and then the children joined hands and danced around the altar singing carols about the Savior's birth.

In 1619, Lancelot Andrewes (1555–1626), the bishop of Winchester, said that Christmas was a day celebrated "as well at home with carols as in the church with anthems."

Young English women of the 16th and 17th centuries would go caroling from house to house during Advent carrying with them a decorated container of some sort that contained a figure of the baby Jesus or the entire Holy Family. In Yorkshire, the women were referred to as "vessel maids." For a coin or a bit of food, they would reveal the figures. Such a container was called a "milly's box" (from "mi'lady's box").

The Crime of Caroling

Martin Luther, the man whose Ninety-five Theses started the whole Protestant Reformation in 1517, was a strong proponent of caroling and used to join with other men in his community and go door to door serenading the neighbors. However, during the period of the Reformation in the 16th and 17th centuries, some of the new Protestant church leaders banned the singing of Christmas carols as a Catholic tradition that did not express sufficient piety.

In 1574, 14 women were brought before the Presbyterian kirk (church) in Aberdeen for the crime of singing carols on Christmas Eve.

In 1583, the Presbyterian kirk in Glasgow ordered the prosecution of anyone caught singing Christmas carols.

In 1588, the church council in Haddington, Scotland, forbade the singing of Christmas carols.

In 1593, the minister at the Presbyterian church in Errol, Scotland, called the singing of Christmas carols a sin equal to that of fornication.

During the Puritan Interregnum of the 1650s in England, caroling was strongly discouraged.

The Church of England banned the use of Christmas carols in worshipping in the mid-17th century. This ban remained in effect until the late 19th century. There were only four carols sanctioned for use at Christmas during this time, including Nahum Tate's "While Shepherds Watched Their Flocks by Night" (see p. 63) and Charles Wesley's "Hark! The Herald Angels Sing" (see p. 66). Christmas carols in general were reintroduced into Anglican church services in 1878 at a Christmas Eve service in Truro, Cornwall.

Even today, the singing of Christmas carols is not welcomed everywhere.

Two major malls in Pensacola, Florida, banned Christmas carols after receiving numerous complaints about the noise they created and the amount of space the singers and their audience took up.

In New York, the Supreme Court upheld a school board's ban of the singing of Christmas carols in 2010.

A number of Canadian schools no longer include the singing of religious Christmas carols in their annual school concerts in December.

DID YOU KNOW?

It is a popular superstition that it is unlucky to sing carols at any time of year other than Christmas.

Keeping Christmas Alive

The Protestant Reformation and especially the Puritan Interregnum led to the demise of the traditional jolly festivities of Christmas in much of England, the main exceptions being those areas furthest removed from the capital—Devon and Cornwall in the west, and Yorkshire in the north. In some parts of England and the American colonies, Christmas ceased to be recognized at all, while in other areas celebrations continued but in a more solemn atmosphere.

The Puritan Parliament's banning of Christmas was a highly contentious issue. Many people did not wish to abandon the merriment of the season, which was seen to be a well-deserved respite from the daily grind of the rest of the year. This feeling was expressed in the anonymous 1653 booklet *Vindication of Christmas*: "Let's dance and sing, and make good cheer, / For Christmas comes but once a year." As early as 1643, the opposing viewpoints are seen in a Royalist ballad, "The World Turned Upside Down," in which people are urged to ignore the laws and celebrate Christmas as usual. In some places, such as Ipswich (1647), Bury St. Edmunds (1646) and Canterbury (1647), there were riots in the streets. In rural areas far removed from London, such as Devon and Cornwall, people curtailed their public celebrations somewhat but still continued with the traditional festivities within their homes. Indeed, it was the religious aspects of the holiday—the special church services—that the Puritans were the most successful at suppressing, resulting in a more secularized holiday both at the time and during the Restoration.

Several people wrote in defense of the holiday and its customary festivities, such as carol singing (a risky venture that often resulted in fines and other penalties). Occasionally, references to carols and caroling can be found in sources between the end of the Puritan Interregnum (1660) and the rise in popularity of caroling throughout England and North America once again in the mid-1800s.

🔔 Thomas Warmstry (1610–1665), an Anglican minister, defended Christmas carol singing in *The Vindication of the Solemnity of the Nativity of Christ* (1648), saying, "Christmas Kariles, if they be such as are fit for the time, and of holy and sober composures, and used with Christian sobriety and purity, are not unlawfull, and may be profitable, if they be sung with grace in the heart."

🔔 Robert Aylett (died 1655) was brave enough to include a Christmas carol at the end of his 1653 *Eclogues and Elegies*.

🔔 Lawrence Price wrote a Christmas book that included several carols in direct opposition to the Cromwellian regime in 1657.

🔔 In his book *In the Twelve Monthes* (1661), M. Stevenson says that caroling with a wassail cup is a part of Christmas festivities.

In *Batt and Batt* (1694), the author speaks of the importance of Christmas cheer, remarking, "Carols, and not minc'd-meat, make Christmas pies."

Historian Henry Bourne (1694–1733) noted in his *Antiquities* (1725) that singing Christmas carols was a common custom, but one of which he did not approve: "to sing it, as is generally done, in the midst of Rioting and Chambering and Wantoness, is…a Scandal to Religion, and a sin against Christ."

In 1745, at the age of 13, George Washington wrote, "Assist me, Muse divine, to sing the Morn, / On Which the Savior of Mankind was born."

In Oliver Goldsmith's novel *The Vicar of Wakefield* (1766), the local parishioners "kept up the Christmas carol."

The Virginia Almanack (1766) stated, "Now Christmas comes, 'tis fit that we / should feast & sing, & merry be."

John Brand, an English antiquarian, wrote that in 1795 children in the northern city of Newcastle-upon-Tyne still went caroling from house to house to wish everyone a happy new year.

The expedition of Meriwether Lewis (1774–1809) and William Clark (1770–1838) began on Christmas Day, 1804, with a volley of gunshots and a song.

Reminiscing about days gone by, essayist Charles Lamb (1775–1834) in *Recollections of Christ's Hospital* (1818) wrote about Christmas at his boarding school: "the carol sung by night at that time of the year, which, when a young boy, I have so often lain awake to hear from seven (the hour of going to bed) till ten when it was sung by the older boys and monitors, and have listened to it, in their rude chanting, till I have been transported in fancy to the fields of Bethlehem, and the song which was sung at the shepherds."

Visiting England in 1820, Washington Irving wrote of his experience of being awoken by a group of carolers in Yorkshire for the first time; he described himself as listening to them with "hushed delight."

Victorian Carol Collections

By the early 19th century, carols and caroling were fast disappearing in England. The official ban on singing Christmas carols in church (except for the four approved hymns), combined with the displacement of families brought about by the Industrial Revolution, made it difficult to keep customs alive.

Some men and women set about searching out and copying down all the carols and folk songs they could find. These were published in collections throughout the 19th century and into the early 20th century. Davies Gilbert, the man who compiled a collection of carols entitled *Some Ancient Christmas Carols (with the tunes to which they were formerly sung in the West of England)* in 1822, believed that carols were a thing of the past. William Sandys, who published *Christmas Carols, Ancient and Modern* in 1833, noted the decline in caroling and offered some suggestions as to why the custom was dying out:

> *In many parts of the kingdom, especially in the northern and western parts, the festival is still kept up with spirit among the middling and lower classes, though its influence is on the wane even with them; the genius of the present age requires work and no play, and since the commencement of this century a great change may be traced. The modern instructors of mankind do not think it necessary to provide popular amusements, considering mental improvement the one thing needful.*

Thomas Wright, author of *Specimens of Old Christmas Carols* (1841) and *Songs and Carols* (1847), scoured old books, broadsheets and manuscripts for Christmas carols to include in his books. These and other published collections of carols acted as a stimulus to reviving the practice of caroling, both door to door and in church, throughout the country.

SONGS OF THE EARLY YEARS

The Boar's Head Carol

The oldest printed English Christmas carol in existence is "The Boar's Head Carol." It is the only song that remains in a collection of carols entitled *Christmasse Carolles* printed by a man named Wynkyn de Worde in 1521. There are several different versions of the carol in use today. The version printed by Wynkyn de Worde is macaronic, with lyrics in both English and Latin.

"The Boar's Head Carol" is associated with Queen's College in Oxford. Every Christmas, an event known as the Boar's Head Gaudy is held there. Today's event varies little from that described in 1607: two scholars dressed in huntsman's cloaks came first, one carrying a spear and the other a sword. Behind them came two pages carrying mustard. Last was the man accorded the honor of carrying in the boar's head. The men sang "The Boar's Head Carol" as they walked, with the whole company joining in on the chorus; they stopped to sing each verse and processed forward when everyone joined in on the refrain. Today, the ceremonial boar's head at Oxford's Queen's College is made from molded jellied meats garnished with rosemary, holly and bay, with an orange placed in its mouth. The main singer is given the orange.

This custom is said to have arisen from a chance encounter between a scholar of the college and a boar in the nearby forest of Shotover. The man was reading a work by Aristotle when he was suddenly attacked by a wild boar. With nothing else to defend himself, he thrust the book down the throat of the charging beast, killing it. He took the body back to the college, where he and his fellows enjoyed a great feast.

The killing of the boar by the young scholar is commemorated in a window at Horspath Parish Church, a village just on the other side of Shotover Forest. The name Copcot appears on the window. No records exist of a Queen's College student by this name. However, another student has been suggested as a possible candidate. Barnard Gilpin (1517–1583) attended the college, and his family's coat-of-arms had a boar on it.

Queen's College, Oxford, is not the only place where boar's head was served in some splendor at the Christmas feast. Sir William Dugdale (1605–1686) recorded that "at the inns of court, during Christmas, the usual dish at the first course at dinner, was a large bore's head, upon a silver platter, with minstralsaye."

It is thought that the tradition of serving a boar's head at important feasts such as Christmas originated with the Vikings, who invaded England repeatedly between the 8th and 11th centuries. While some of the invaders came simply to seize plunder, many others came as settlers. These Viking settlers brought their customs and religious beliefs with them, including the practice of sacrificing a boar to Freyja, the Norse goddess of fertility, on the Winter Solstice. This custom survived for a long time in areas of northern England, such as Yorkshire, that had been heavily set-tled by the Vikings. The practice was simply shifted over a few days to Christmas when the settlers converted to Christianity. It is possible that students from the area took the custom with them when they went to Oxford to study. Queen's College is known to have had many students from northern England.

Another boar's head carol that survives is "The Exeter Boar's Head Carol." It was written by Richard Smert (1428–1477), a Devonshire priest who served as vicar-choral of Exeter Cathedral for many years. Smert loved Christmas and wrote sev-eral songs to celebrate the season. "The Exeter Boar's Head Carol" is unique in that the boar's head is used as a symbol for Christ.

The custom of processing with a boar's head at Christmastime is practiced at Notting Hill and Ealing High School in London, but the head is made from paper maché. Across the Atlantic, Renaissance boar's head festivals are becoming increasingly pop-ular at churches and colleges throughout Texas during the Christmas season.

DID YOU KNOW?

A British Christmas stamp from 1978 featured "The Boar's Head Carol."

Rosemary
One line of "The Boar's Head Carol" describes the boar's head on the platter as "bedecked with bays and rosemary." Rosemary, a common herb, has its own legend attached to it.

Rosemary was named for the Virgin Mary. The medieval legend stated that Mary wore a white cloak when the family fled to Egypt. Once, when they stopped, she laid the cloak on some rosemary bushes, which turned the cloak purple.

The Twelve Days of Christmas

The popular Christmas carol "The Twelve Days of Christmas" is a song in which additional gifts are added for each day/verse. In the 19th century, "The Twelve Days of Christmas" was played on the evenings of the twelve days of Christmas as a memory-and-forfeits game. One player would start by singing the first verse. This would be repeated by each player. Then the second verse would be added and so on. Every time a player forgot a verse, a fine or forfeit was demanded.

Traditional English and Sussex Versions

"The Twelve Days of Christmas" is a very old carol dating back to at least the 16th century. In the traditional song, the gifts given by the lover are a partridge in a pear tree, two turtledoves, three French hens, four calling birds, five golden rings, six geese a-laying, seven swans a-swimming, eight maids a-milking, nine ladies dancing, ten lords a-leaping, eleven pipers piping and twelve drummers drumming, for a grand total of 364 gifts by the twelfth day! In the Sussex version, there are four canaries, eight deer a-running, ten ladies skipping, eleven bears a-baiting and twelve parsons preaching.

French Version

An early French version of "The Twelve Days of Christmas" focused on the feasting involved in the Yuletide celebrations. In this version, the lover bestows upon his true love one good stuffing without bones, two breasts of veal, three joints of beef, four pigs' trotters, five legs of mutton, six partridges with cabbage, seven spitted rabbits, eight plates of salad, nine dishes from the chapterhouse, ten full casks, eleven beautiful maidens and twelve musketeers with swords. Clearly, he was not concerned about his lady love being supermodel thin.

Canadian Hoser Version

A more modern version of the song was performed by the
Canadian comedians known as the McKenzie brothers. Bob and
Doug McKenzie (played by Rick Moranis and Dave Thomas) are
the hosers of the Great White North skit on the comedy *SCTV*.
Their version of "The Twelve Days of Christmas" included gifts
of eight comic books, five golden tuques and a beer in a tree.

New Zealand and Australian Versions

Other places in the world have altered the song's lyrics to fit the
local landscape better. For example, the New Zealand version
of "The Twelve Days of Christmas" begins with "a pukeko in
a ponga tree." In the Australian version of "The Twelve Days of
Christmas," the list of gifts is a bell bird in a flametree, two wal-
labies, three lorikeets, four pelicans, five crocodiles, six penguins
peeping, seven mice a-marching, eight quokkas cooking, nine
wombats knitting, ten dingoes dancing, eleven lizards leaping,
and twelve koalas clowning. Another version substitutes seven
emus running and a kookaburra in a gum tree.

Hawaiian Version

The Hawaiian version of the song is called "Numbah One Day of Christmas." It was written in pidgin English in 1959 by Eaton Magoon Jr., Edward Kenny and Gordon Phelps. The gifts include "one mynah bird in a papaya tree," "five beeg fat peegs," poi, ukeleles and hula lessons.

DID YOU  KNOW?

In 567, the Council of Tours (a meeting of church leaders to decide on church doctrine and practice) declared the period of 12 days between the Nativity (December 25) and Epiphany (January 6) of Christ to be a festive season. The custom of having 12 extraordinary days following the Winter Solstice was an ancient one that stemmed from the different number of days in a year when calculated based on the sun (365¼) and on the moon (354).

Catholic Symbolism Behind "The Twelve Days of Christmas"

It has long been believed that the carol "The Twelve Days of Christmas" was developed as a way of teaching Catholic theology during the turbulent years of the 16th and 17th centuries in England. During this time, the kingdom's religion switched numerous times, generally with each new monarch. Then the Civil War of the mid-17th century brought in a decade of Puritan rule. It was a dangerous time to be a Catholic in England. Nonetheless, many people remained loyal to their pre-Reformation faith. Priests came from the Continent to preach in the homes of Catholic gentry. Many secret places of worship were established throughout the country.

Children were taught the beliefs of their parents in a number of covert ways. To be openly Catholic could result in loss of property or even death by burning at the stake. The singing of "The

Twelve Days of Christmas" may have been a way of both teaching the catechism and letting Catholic recusants identify each other. The following is a list of the supposedly hidden Catholic meanings behind the words of this popular carol.

My true love (i.e., God) gave to me…

🔔 a partridge in a pear tree. The partridge is the only bird that will die to save the lives of its chicks and was thus said to represent Jesus; the pear tree symbolized the cross upon which Christ died.

🔔 two turtledoves. Doves, associated with truth and peace, stood for the Old and New Testaments of the Bible.

🔔 three French hens. There are two theories as to what exactly these three birds signified: either the gifts of the three Magi (i.e., gold, frankincense and myrrh) or the gifts of faith, hope and love as mentioned in 1 Corinthians 13:13.

🔔 four calling birds. These birds symbolized the authors of the four Gospels (i.e., Matthew, Mark, Luke and John) who "called out" the tale of Jesus' life.

🔔 five golden rings. These costly treasures represented the first five books of the Old Testament, known as the Pentateuch by Christians or the Torah by Jews.

🔔 six geese a-laying. The new life being created by these six geese stood for the new world created by God in six days.

🔔 seven swans a-swimming. These beautiful birds signified the seven gifts of the Holy Spirit as listed in Isaiah 11:2–3: prophecy, service, teaching, encouraging, giving, leadership and mercy.

🔔 eight maids a-milking. Milkmaids were low in the rigid social hierarchy of the period and thus were well chosen to represent those who are mentioned in Matthew 53:10 as being blessed: the poor in spirit, those who mourn, the meek, the hungry, the merciful, the pure of heart, the peacemakers and the righteous.

nine ladies dancing. These were the nine fruits of the Spirit listed in 1 Corinthians 12:7–11: love, joy, peace, patience, kindness, goodness, faithfulness, gentleness and self-control.

ten lords a-leaping. Lords, the representatives and enforcers of the laws of the land, served to represent the laws given by God to Moses—the Ten Commandments.

eleven pipers piping. These pipers were the eleven faithful disciples who spread Jesus' message.

twelve drummers drumming. They represented the twelve different parts of the Apostles' Creed.

O Christmas Tree

Various versions of "O Christmas Tree" (*O Tannenbaum*) have been sung in German-speaking areas since at least 1550. The most well-known version was written by Ernst Anschütz in 1824. "O Christmas Tree" is popular in Germany and North America but is rarely heard in England.

The Irish playwright George Bernard Shaw (1856–1950) did not like the tune of "O Christmas Tree," saying it sounded like "the funeral march of a dead eel." Others must disagree; the melody has been appropriated for numerous songs, including the British Labour Party's "Red Flag," Cornell University's "Evening Song," Maryland's "Maryland, My Maryland," and Iowa's "The Song of Iowa."

"O Christmas Tree" was played in the 1988 movie *Ernest Saves Christmas*.

Caroling and the Christmas Tree

People have decorated their homes during the long winter months with evergreen plants of all sorts for thousands of years. The custom of bringing an evergreen tree into the house and decorating it for the festive season originated in Germany and spread out from there, largely through the intermarriage of members of the German aristocracy with the royal families of Europe. Today, it is inconceivable for most people in the Western World to think of celebrating Christmas without their beloved tree and holiday music. These two symbols of the holiday have been combined in numerous ways.

🔔 During the Christmas season, Londoners gather in Trafalgar Square to sing carols while gathered around a large Christmas tree. The tree is an annual gift from the people of Oslo, Norway, for the help they received from Britain during World War II.

🔔 Christmas tree choirs are popular in the U.S., where choir members dress in green cloaks and stand in a tree formation to perform. A star is placed at the top.

🔔 In Indonesia, people on their way to Midnight Mass begin to sing carols when they see the few twinkling lights of the church's Christmas tree. As they draw nearer singing, more candles are lit until the whole tree is aglow.

🔔 On Christmas Eve in Norway, following the visit of Julesvenn, the Norwegian gift-giver, people join hands around the Christmas tree and then walk around it, singing carols.

🔔 Since 1945, Park Avenue in New York City has featured a Christmas tree display in memory of those killed in World War II. A lighting ceremony is held each year on the first Sunday of December at the Brick Church on 91 Street and Park Avenue. Christmas carols and "Taps" (a funeral song used by the U.S. military) are played at this event.

In Lithuania, everyone gathers around the Christmas tree to sing songs on Christmas Eve, following the breaking and sharing of wafers.

Some of the American presidents' Christmas tree themes have been musical. For example, the Kennedys' Nutcracker Suite tree with decorations made by blind and elderly artisans; and the Clintons' Twelve Days of Christmas tree with decorations done by art students.

In Slovakia and the Czech Republic, someone rings a bell when the first star has been spotted on Christmas Eve. Everyone then gathers in a room to see the Christmas tree and manger scene that has been hidden there until that moment. Everyone kneels and says a prayer. This is followed by carol singing.

Deck the Halls

"Deck the Halls" is a traditional Welsh Christmas carol, dating from the 16th century or earlier. It is composed in the style of a circle dance and was meant to be sung while dancing: "follow me in merry measure." The carolers would dance in a circle, sometimes to the accompaniment of a harpist. Each person would contribute a verse, often composed on the spot. If the person was unable to do so, they would sit down. In between the verses, the harpist would play a short refrain allowing the singers a short respite to think up a new verse. If no harpist was present, the people would sing nonsense words, the "fa-la-la-la-la" section of the song.

🔔 The traditional Welsh version of "Deck the Halls" was sung and danced on New Year's Eve.

🔔 The English translation of "Deck the Halls" is nothing like the Welsh original except for the reference to the ending of one year and the beginning of another.

🔔 Clifton Siple wrote a parody of "Deck the Halls" in 1970 that went, "Deck the halls with marijuana fa-la-la-la-la-la-la-la-la, / 'Tis the time to reach nirvana fa-la-la-la-la-la-la-la-la…"

The Holly and the Ivy

The first record of the carol "The Holly and the Ivy" is from 1710, when it was printed in an English broadside. The text and tune for "The Holly and the Ivy" were collected by Cecil Sharp from Mary Clayton of Chipping Camden, Gloucestershire, and published in *English Folk-Carols* in 1911.

Holly Caroling Customs

A caroling custom from the Exmoor region of England was for groups of singers to ride from farm to farm carrying lanterns and wearing hats decorated with sprigs of holly. They were known as "holly riders." They would stop and sing at each farm, and were given a few coins or some cider and treats in return.

In Westmoreland, carolers used to carry a decorated holly tree attached to a pole along with torches when they went about from house to house on Twelfth Night singing Christmas songs.

Holly Lore

Holly has played a central role in the spiritual practices and folk customs and beliefs of the people living in the British Isles since time immemorial. Holly is one of the few plants that retains its greenery throughout the cold, dark winter months, and its bright berries bring a burst of color and life to an otherwise dreary and dead environment. Not surprisingly, it has long been a popular decoration during that time.

The Romans celebrated a midwinter festival called the Saturnalia in which they used sprigs of holly to decorate their homes as well as sending it to friends as a sign of good will and best wishes.

In some parts of England, a sprig of holly was saved and then burned after the rest of the Christmas greenery was taken down. This sprig of holly was thought to provide protection against witches, demons, thunder, lightning and the Evil Eye for the coming year.

The holly tree was known to medieval monks as the Holy tree because of its reputed ability to ward off evil spirits.

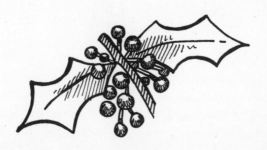

🔔 The Germans called holly "Christ's dorn" (i.e., thorn). They believed that it was used to make the crown of thorns worn by Jesus on his way to the Crucifixion. The berries, they thought, were stained red by the blood of Christ. The plant's white blossoms were said to represent His purity.

🔔 In Cornwall, holly used to be known as "Aunt Mary's tree" because of its association with the Virgin Mary.

🔔 Holly was also considered to be a symbol of love because of its clinging nature.

🔔 It was believed that if holly was brought into the house before Christmas Eve, quarrels would break out among the family members. If you remove the holly from the house before Epiphany, it will bring three times that amount of bad luck.

🔔 In England, the first person to enter a house on New Year's Day should carry a sprig of holly to bring good fortune to the household. After the holidays are over, this sprig of holly should be burned.

🔔 It is unlucky to carry a flowering sprig of holly into a house.

🔔 It is unlucky to stomp on holly berries.

Ivy Beliefs

Not only holly but also ivy was the subject of many superstitious beliefs of our British forebears.

🔔 Holly was long associated with maleness and goodness while ivy was linked to femaleness and evil.

🔔 In Oxfordshire, a man who failed to provide a maiden with ivy for holiday decorating was likely to find his breeches nailed to the outside of her house. In Wiltshire, a similarly negligent man would be refused the customary Christmas greeting of a kiss.

In some areas of Britain, ivy leaves were fed to the cattle between the morning milk and noon on Christmas Day to keep the Devil away.

 A common custom in England was to place an ivy leaf in a bowl of water on New Year's Eve and leave it there till the Eve of Twelfth Night. The condition of the leaf foretold the person's health in the coming year. A green leaf meant good health. A spotted leaf indicated either impending illness or death; spots all over meant death but fewer spots meant illness, with the location of the spots corresponding to areas of the person's body (e.g., top of the leaf = the head, etc.).

The Huron Carol

"The Huron Carol" (or "Jesus Ahatonhia") is the only carol originally written in a Native American language that has come to be known around the world. It is believed to have been written by a Jesuit missionary named Jean de Brébeuf during his years (1626–1629 and 1634–1649) working with the Hurons in the Great Lakes region of Canada. The Hurons gave Brébeuf the name Echom.

In 1642, Brébeuf noted in his writings that the Hurons felt a special devotion to Christmas and were captivated by the story of Jesus' birth. They had built a small chapel of cedar and fir branches wherein they had set up a manger. They would travel a great distance to come to this chapel to worship and sing hymns of praise on Christmas. One of these songs was "The Huron Carol," sung to the tune of a contemporary French folk song, *Une Jeune Pucelle*. Another Jesuit priest, Father Barthélémy Vimont, recorded in 1645 that the Hurons at Mackinac (now Mackinaw, Michigan) also met at Christmas to sing carols in honor of the Christ Child.

In the late 1640s, the Hurons were attacked by their long-time enemies, the Iroquois. The attack was devastating and long-lasting, killing a majority of the Huron people. Brébeuf refused to leave the people to whom he had ministered for so many years. He was captured, tortured and burned at the stake by the Iroquois in 1649.

When he wrote "The Huron Carol," Brébeuf made some changes to the traditional Christmas story to make it comprehensible to his Native audience. For example, God became Gitchi Manitou; the Wise Men became chiefs; shepherds became hunters; swaddling clothes became "a ragged robe of rabbit skin"; gold, frankincense and myrrh became fox and beaver pelts; and the stable became a lodge.

"The Huron Carol" was preserved in the oral tradition of the Hurons at Lorette in Quebec. A century later it was written down by Father de Villeneuve. The best-known English translation of "The Huron Carol" was done by Jesse Edgar Middleton in 1926. The carol was the subject of three Canadian Christmas stamps issued in 1977.

I Saw Three Ships

One of the stranger popular Christmas carols of old is "I Saw Three Ships." The song speaks of three ships that come sailing into Bethlehem on Christmas morning. This is quite a feat because Bethlehem is, and always has been, a land-locked town.

It is thought that the song refers to the arrival of three human skulls at Cologne in 1162. This theory is backed up by a reference to this event in the earliest existing copy of the carol in John Forbes' second edition of *Cantus, Songs & Fancies* (1666).

The three skulls were believed to be those of the three Magi who visited Jesus shortly after his birth in Bethlehem. The story goes that the Roman empress Helena, mother of Constantine the Great, who in 313 made it legal to practice Christianity within the Roman Empire, discovered the remains of the three Magi on her trip to the Holy Land in 326–328. (She is also credited with finding the remains of the True Cross, as well as the sites of Jesus' birth and ascension into Heaven.) These remains were later taken by St. Eustathius from Constantinople to Milan.

In 1162, the Holy Roman Emperor Frederick Barbarossa decided to give the skulls from these three skeletons as a gift to the cathedral in Cologne. Such a gift would have been very lucrative, as people in the Middle Ages traveled great distances to sites believed to be of religious importance, either because of an event that occurred there or because of the holy relics said to be housed there. These pilgrims spent a great deal of money on lodgings, food and souvenirs. Renaldus, the bishop of Cologne, is said to have traveled by ship with these skulls from Milan to Cologne. They can still be found in Cologne Cathedral in a trio of jeweled caskets.

So it is this final journey aboard ship from Milan to Cologne that is said to have been the inspiration behind the carol "I Saw Three Ships." Whatever the true story behind this old carol, it was put into its modern arrangement by Sir John Stainer (1840–1901), an English composer and organist.

 Nat King Cole recorded the song in 1960. Sting sang the carol for the multiple-artist collection *A Very Special Christmas* in 1989.

County Carols

Some carols are associated with particular regions, either because they were written in the area or because through historical chance they have only survived there.

The Wexford Carol
"The Wexford Carol" is a traditional Irish hymn dating back to about the 12th century. The song was passed down through the years in Enniscorthy, County Wexford. Julie Andrews (1966), Loreena McKennitt (1987), the Chieftains (1991) and Celtic Woman (2006) are among the many artists who have recorded the song. It is one of Julie Andrews' favorite Christmas songs. Local tradition stated that the carol could be sung by men only.

The Gloucestershire Wassail
This song has been sung in the Gloucestershire county of England for centuries. Farmers go out into their apple orchards, usually on New Year's Eve, and offer a toast and a song to the trees in hopes of obtaining a good crop in the coming year. The exact age of this song is unknown, but it is likely of medieval origin. It was first published in the *Oxford Book of Carols* in 1928.

The Sussex Carol
This song is popular in Britain, though not well known in North America. It was first published in 1684 by Luke Waddinge, an Irish bishop, in *A Small Garland of Pious and Godly Songs*. It is known as "The Sussex Carol" because the lyrics and tune used

today were recorded in the early 20th century as sung by Harriet Verrall of Monk's Gate, Sussex. The carol has been set to music by many composers. It is often used in King's College's Festival of Nine Lessons and Carols.

The Worcestershire Carol

Both the lyrics and the music for this carol were written by the Anglican minister William Henry Havergal (1793–1870). He called the hymn "How Grand and How Bright." The song was written in 1827, but it was not published until 1858 in a collection entitled *Fireside Music*. It was also printed and distributed on broadsheets throughout the county of Worcestershire, where it became quite popular for a while and gained the name "The Worcestershire Carol." One man from Slimbridge, Worcestershire, named Ray Lord loved the song, which had been passed down orally in his family, so much that when he died, the first line of it was carved onto his tombstone.

The Kilmore Carols

Kilmore is a small rural community located in County Wexford in the southeast of Ireland. For nearly three centuries, a tradition of Christmas caroling has been passed down in Kilmore. The songs have been passed down orally from generation to generation of men in the area. Each year, a group of six of these men sings the carols during the twelve days of Christmas.

The tradition seems to have started with the placement of William Devereux (1696–1771) as priest of St. Mary's Church in Kilmore. In 1728, he published a booklet of hymns entitled *A New Garland Containing Songs for Christmas*. He appears to have been the author of several of the Kilmore carols, also copying a few by an earlier writer and bishop, Luke Waddinge (died 1688), that had previously been published in *A Small Garland of Pious and Godly Songs* in 1684.

The Kilmore carolers have so far resisted recording their carols. The six men divide into two groups of three to sing alternating verses. There is no instrumental accompaniment and the songs are sung only in St. Mary's Church during Communion. There has always been a member of the local Devereux family among the singers.

The Kilmore carols are very dark. Over the years, various priests have discouraged people from singing them. Some of the priests were successful in their endeavors, and the carols died out in the surrounding towns, remaining in use only at St. Mary's in Kilmore.

Each of the 13 Kilmore carols is sung on a specific day during the twelve days of Christmas. "The Darkest Midnight" is sung at Midnight Mass on Christmas Eve. Christmas Day is welcomed with the aptly named "Christmas Day Has Come," followed by "Ye Sons of Men With Me Rejoice," "An Angel This Night" and "A Virgin Queen in Bethlehem." On December 26, St. Stephen's Day, "A Carol for Holy Innocence" is sung. The following day is heard "A Carol for the Feast of St. John." December 28 is Holy Innocents Day, commemorating the slaughter of baby boys in Israel by King Herod's soldiers. In Kilmore, the event is recognized in the carol "Hail Ye Flowers of Martyrs." "This Feast of Saint Sylvester Well Deserves a Song" is sung by the men on December 29. New Year's Day has two songs: "Sweetest of All Names, Jesus" and "To Greet Our Savior's Dear One." "Jerusalem, Our Happy Home" and "Now to Conclude Our Christmas Mirth" are the final carols of the cycle.

DID YOU KNOW?

President Theodore Roosevelt's favorite Christmas carol was one that was sung only at Christ Church at Oyster Bay. It is called "Christmas on the Sea." It was recorded by Burl Ives in 1972.

SONGS IN THE HYMNAL

While Shepherds Watched Their Flocks by Night

"While Shepherds Watched Their Flocks by Night" was written by Nahum Tate (1652–1715), later England's Poet Laureate, circa 1696. The lyrics are a paraphrase of Luke 2:8–14.

"While Shepherds Watched Their Flocks by Night" was approved as a hymn by the Anglican Church in 1700. It was the only approved carol until "Hark! The Herald Angels Sing" was added in 1782.

"While Shepherds Watched Their Flocks by Night" has been set to more than 100 different tunes, the most commonly sung of which is "Winchester Old," a psalm tune first published in 1592.

Thomas Hardy's Carol

Thomas Hardy (1840–1928) was an English poet and novelist, known for such works as *Tess of the d'Urbervilles* and *The Mayor of Casterbridge*. His ashes are buried in Westminster Abbey's Poets' Corner, but his heart is buried in the same grave as his first wife,

Emma. Hardy mentioned the Christmas carol "While Shepherds Watched Their Flocks by Night" in several pieces of his writing.

In *Tess of the d'Urbervilles*, William Dewy calms an enraged bull by playing "the Nativity hymn" on his fiddle. The nativity hymn referred to was "While Shepherds Watched Their Flocks by Night."

In Hardy's poem "The Dead Quire," the sound of "While Shepherds Watched Their Flocks by Night" stops the Christmas Eve drinking and carousing of a group of young men of Dorset.

The Devil and his demon minions are overcome by the tune of "While Shepherds Watched Their Flocks by Night" in Hardy's poem "The Paphian Ball."

Thomas Hardy's father William included part of the tune for "While Shepherds Watched Their Flocks by Night" in a carol book he compiled. Interestingly, he was a model for William Dewy in *Tess of the d'Urbervilles*.

DID YOU KNOW?

In Italy, children dress up like shepherds and go door to door singing carols on December 23.

Joy to the World

"Joy to the World," one of the most popular Christmas songs ever, was never intended to be a Christmas song. The lyricist, Isaac Watts (1674–1748), was referring to the coming of the Lord at the end of the world, not Christ's birth at Bethlehem. This is why there is no direct reference to Christmas in the song. Both the Seventh-Day Adventists and the Mormons have changed the words to reflect the original meaning, "The Lord is come" becoming "The Lord will come."

"Joy to the World" first appeared in 1719 in Isaac Watts' *The Psalms of David*. It is based upon Psalm 98.

In 1839, American Lowell Mason (1792–1872) composed the music—or stole the score from German composer George Frideric Handel (1685–1759). Mason wrote that he took the score from Handel, but modern scholars can find no evidence for this. The tune is called "Antioch," named for the Syrian city in which the term "Christian" was first used to describe the followers of Jesus Christ.

"Joy to the World" was the favorite Christmas song of the second American president, John Adams.

Between 1874 and 1940, "Joy to the World" was in the general hymns section of Episcopalian hymnals.

The Nazi government would not allow "Joy to the World" to be played on the radio in Austria, beginning in 1938.

"Joy to the World" is the last Christmas carol sung by the children in *A Charlie Brown Christmas* (1965). This scene was featured on a 2003 Christmas stamp from Gibraltar.

In 2001, the island of St. Helena paid tribute on its Christmas stamps to singer Tammy Wynette (1942–1998) and carols she recorded, including "Joy to the World."

Other singers who have recorded the song include the Supremes, Boney M, Whitney Houston, Mariah Carey, Faith Hill, Clay Aiken and the Jonas Brothers.

Isaac Watts: Hymn Writer Extraordinaire

The father of Isaac Watts did not conform to the state religion of England, practicing a more extreme form of Protestantism, and was jailed twice as a result. Watts' mother would carry her young son with her to sing hymns at the prison gate to keep up her husband's spirits.

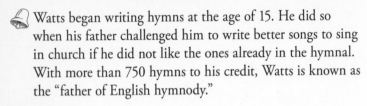 Watts began writing hymns at the age of 15. He did so when his father challenged him to write better songs to sing in church if he did not like the ones already in the hymnal. With more than 750 hymns to his credit, Watts is known as the "father of English hymnody."

Watts was a small man, standing barely over five feet tall.

He became a minister and gave his first sermon on his 21st birthday.

In 1724, Watts wrote a book on logic that became the standard textbook on the subject at Cambridge and Oxford for the next century. Ironically, Watts' non-conformity had prevented him from being allowed to study at either school.

Watts was invited to visit his friends Sir Thomas and Lady Mary Abney for a week in 1712. He never left. Instead, he remained living with them until his death 36 years later.

Hark! The Herald Angels Sing

"Hark! The Herald Angels Sing" was written in 1739 by Charles Wesley (1707–1788). It is the most popular of the numerous hymns written by Charles Wesley, brother of the founder of Methodism, John Wesley.

When Charles Wesley's college friend George Whitefield (1714–1770) published Wesley's new Christmas hymn, he changed the first line from the original "Hark! How all the welkin rings!" ("welkin" being a medieval term for "sky" or "firmament") to "Hark! The herald angels sing." Whitefield felt that Wesley's line sounded too archaic, but his change infuriated Wesley because nowhere in the Bible does it say anything about angels singing at Jesus' birth.

The hymn was further altered by Martin Mandan, John Kempthorne and several others. In 1760, Mandan changed the second part of verse two from "Universal nature say / Christ the Lord is born today," to "With the angelic hosts proclaim / Christ is born in Bethlehem!" The 1861 *Hymns Ancient and Modern* changed two lines of verse four from "Pleased as man with men to appear / Jesus, our Immanuel here" to "Pleased as man with man to dwell / Jesus, our Immanuel."

In 1782, "Hark! The Herald Angels Sing" became the second carol authorized to be sung in the Anglican Church. The first had been "While Shepherds Watched Their Flocks by Night."

In 1855, the English musician W.H. Cummings adapted part of Felix Mendelssohn's 1840 cantata to the words of "Hark! The Herald Angels Sing." This music had earlier been used for the aria "Thus When Mars from Wars Returning" in the 1715 opera *Venus and Adonis* by Johann Christoph Pepusch (1667–1752).

The phrase "sun of righteousness" comes from the prophet Malachi, who referred to the Messiah thus.

"Hark! The Herald Angels Sing" is generally the recessional hymn for King's College's Festival of Nine Lessons and Carols.

"Come, Thou Long-Expected Jesus" is another Christmas hymn written by Wesley. It was first published in 1744 in his *Hymns for the Nativity of Our Lord*. It is sung to the tune "Hyfrydol," composed by Welshman Rowland Prichard (1811–1887) in 1855.

DID YOU KNOW?

Charles Wesley wrote more than 6000 hymns.

The Carol in Popular Culture

In the classic Christmas movie *It's a Wonderful Life* (1946), "Hark! The Herald Angels Sing" plays in the background during the ending of the war.

On his 1959 album, *An Evening Wasted with Tom Lehrer*, the singer-songwriter satirizes the commercialism of the modern Christmas in the song "A Christmas Carol." Included in the song are the lines "Hark the herald tribune sings, / Advertising wondrous things."

In the animated classic *A Charlie Brown Christmas* (1965), Charlie Brown, Linus, Lucy and all the gang join together to hum "Hark! The Herald Angels Sing."

In 1988, Nauru produced a Christmas stamp with the musical score for the first two bars of "Hark! The Herald Angels Sing" and the accompanying words in both English and the local language, Nauruan.

People gather around the piano and sing "Hark! The Herald Angels Sing" at the Christmas party in the 1995 movie *Jumanji*.

"'Tis the Fifteenth Season" (2003) is the seventh Christmas special of *The Simpsons*. After Homer and Ned get into a competition to see who the nicest guy in town is, Homer steals everyone's presents thinking people would be happier without these material possessions. After returning the gifts to his angry neighbors, everyone joins Homer in singing "Hark! The Herald Angels Sing." The song is featured in two other episodes of *The Simpsons*: "Treehouse of Horror IV" (1993) and "The Fight before Christmas" (2010).

"Hark! The Herald Angels Sing" is heard on the 2009 Disney version of *A Christmas Carol* when the Ghost of Christmas Present visits Scrooge.

In 2011, at the 30th Annual Christmas in Washington, President Barack Obama and his family joined stars such as Justin Bieber and Jennifer Hudson in singing "Hark! The Herald Angels Sing."

DID YOU KNOW?

King Edward VIII of England abdicated on December 10, 1936. Some cockney carol-singers took to singing "Hark! the herald angels sing, Missis Simpson's pinched our King!"

Adeste Fideles

John Francis Wade (1711–1786), an English Roman Catholic resident of Douai, France, is believed to have written "Adeste Fideles" sometime between 1740 and 1744. Wade is also responsible for composing the music for this song. He first published "Adeste Fideles" in *Cantus Diversi* ("Diverse Songs") in 1751.

🔔 Wade was originally from Lancashire in northern England, an area that retained the tradition of caroling.

🔔 Wade wrote four verses of "Adeste Fideles." Abbé Etienne Borderies (1764–1832) added three more in 1794. Another verse was later added by an unknown person.

🔔 "Adeste Fideles" was originally known as "The Portuguese Hymn" in England because it was introduced into the country in the late 18th century via the Portuguese Embassy.

🔔 An Anglican minister, Frederick Oakeley (1802–1880), translated "Adeste Fideles" as "Ye Faithful, Approach Ye" in 1841. Eleven years later, after his conversion to Roman Catholicism, Oakeley produced a second translation, the one we know today: "O Come, All Ye Faithful."

🔔 "Adeste Fideles" was one of President Dwight Eisenhower's (1890–1969) favorite Christmas carols, the other two being "Silent Night" and "The First Noël."

🔔 Bing Crosby, though at first reluctant to record a religious song, eventually came to sing "Adeste Fideles" as the opening number on his Christmas show every year. Crosby would sing the chorus in Latin and then audience members would join in to sing it in English.

🔔 Many singers and musical groups have recorded the song, including the rather unlikely band Twisted Sister.

🔔 "O Come, All Ye Faithful" can be heard playing at Tezo's house on the 2008 movie *Pride and Glory*.

Adeste Fideles: The Jacobite Carol?
John Francis Wade was a supporter of the Jacobite cause. His manuscript ornamentation is full of symbols of his allegiance. It

has even been suggested that "Adeste Fideles" is actually a rallying cry for supporters of the Old Pretender, James Stuart (1688–1766), and the unsuccessful Jacobite Uprising of 1745. For example, *adeste fideles* was "come faithful Jacobites" and *venite in Bethlehem* was "come to Bethlehem" (i.e., England).

Silent Night

Undoubtedly the most popular religious Christmas carol is the Austrian melody "Silent Night, Holy Night" (*Stille Nacht, Heilige Nacht*). It is sung in churches worldwide on Christmas Eve and is heard repeatedly throughout the holiday season. So what is the story behind this well-known tune?

Joseph Mohr (1792–1848), a village priest in Oberndorf, Austria, wrote the lyrics to "Silent Night" in 1816. The story goes that two years later, in 1818, when he realized that the organ in his small rural church was in need of repair and would not be available for use at the Christmas Eve service, Mohr brought the words to Franz Gruber (1787–1863), who composed guitar music for the carol.

Since then, "Silent Night" has been translated into over 300 languages. Its English version was written in 1863 by the Episcopalean minister John Freeman Young.

In 1948, Austria produced a stamp to mark the 130th anniversary of the first performance of "Silent Night." Pictured on it were the song's writer and composer. In 1958, Austria produced a Christmas stamp showing the village church where "Silent Night" was first sung. Also that year, to mark the 140th anniversary of that event, the country's postmark depicted the carol's opening bars. The 1968 Austrian stamp celebrating the 150th anniversary of the carol depicted the nativity scene from the memorial chapel at Oberndorf.

🔔 Gruber's father was a linen weaver who did not like his son wasting his time playing music, so Franz had to study music in secret with the choirmaster and organist of the local church.

🔔 "Silent Night" was first known as "The Tyrolean Folk Song" by many people.

🔔 "Silent Night" was the most popular Chistmas carol in 19th-century Germany among both Catholics and Protestants. Christmas Eve services in Germany usually end with the singing of "Silent Night" or "O Happy, O Blessed Christmas."

🔔 "Silent Night" highlights the 19th-century bourgeois ideal of "mother and child."

🔔 In Austria, "Silent Night" is protected from commercialism and is thus neither played, broadcast nor sung until Christmas Eve. The chapel in the Austrian village of Oberndorf, where the carol originated, is a popular spot for tourists to attend Midnight Mass.

🔔 In 2000, historian Bill Egan was awarded the Gold Medal of Honor of the Republic of Austria for his research on the Christmas carol "Silent Night."

🔔 In Oberndorf, Austria, is the only museum in the world devoted to a Christmas carol—the Silent Night Museum.

"Silent Night" was the favorite Christmas song of the Prussian Kaiser Frederick Wilhelm IV (1795–1861) and American presidents Lyndon B. Johnson (1908–1973) and Ronald Reagan (1911–2004).

The first country Christmas recording of "Silent Night" was Roy Rogers' version in 1940.

Performer Bob Hope hosted an annual Christmas special for 17 years. At the end of each one, he sang "Silent Night."

Polish composer Krzysztof Penderecki's "Second Symphony," written in 1979–1980, makes extensive use of quotations from "Silent Night." It is sometimes referred to as his Christmas symphony.

In 1989, Enya recorded a version of "Silent Night" in Gaelic—*Oíche Chiúin*. In 2009, Andrea Bocelli recorded "Silent Night" in Italian—*Noche de Paz*.

"Silent Night" has appeared in films many times, including *The Nativity Story* (2006), *The Badge* (2002), *Deuces Wild* (2002), *Forrest Gump* (1994), *Gods and Generals* (2003), *L.A. Confidential* (1997), *Love Actually* (2003), *One Hour Photo* (2002), *Saved!* (2004) and *Sweet Hearts Dance* (1998).

"Silent Night" has also featured quite frequently on television, including episodes of *Haven*, *NCIS*, *Grey's Anatomy* and *Chuck*. Pampers used Cyndi Lauper's recording of "Silent Night" in one of its commercials.

DID YOU KNOW?

In 2003, labor unions in Austria, the country that gave birth to the carol "Silent Night," demanded that stores limit the playing of Christmas carols to one hour a day, calling their constant playing "psychological terrorism."

Angelic Voices Singing

Angels from the Realms of Glory

"Angels from the Realms of Glory" was written by the radical journalist and hymn writer James Montgomery (1771–1854). It first appeared in print in the English newspaper the *Sheffield Iris* on December 24, 1816. Henry Smart (1813–1879), a blind organist, wrote the music for the carol.

As a young man, James Montgomery was expelled from a Moravian seminary for his obsessive poetry writing. As an adult, Montgomery served time in prison twice for his political views. The first time was as a supporter of the French Revolution. The second was for supporting a local reform riot in Sheffield.

"Angels from the Realms of Glory" appeared in a hymnal made for the congregation at London's Regent Square Presbyterian Church in 1867, earning it an alternate title of "The Regent Square Carol." It is also known as "The Westminster Carol."

"Angels from the Realms of Glory" is one of three hymns traditionally sung at Midnight Mass on Christmas Eve in Ireland. The other two hymns are "Silent Night" and "Adeste Fideles."

Angels We Have Heard on High

"Angels We Have Heard on High" is a combination of an ancient gloria—a short, repetitive song of praise traditionally sung at Christmas services—and a French carol called "Angels in our Fields" (*Les Ange dans nos Campagnes*). Both parts are old, with the French carol dating back to at least the 18th century, and of unknown origin. James Chadwick (1813–1882), a Roman Catholic bishop of Hexham and Newcastle, translated the French lyrics of "Angels We Have Heard on High" to English in 1862.

Protestants sometimes change the last two lines of the final verse ("Mary, Joseph, lend your aid / While our hearts in love we raise") to make them less intercessory ("Lend your voices, lend your aid / To proclaim the Savior's birth").

DID YOU KNOW?

The word "angel" comes from the Greek word *angelos*, meaning "messenger" or "herald."

O Holy Night

"O Holy Night" (*Cantique de Noël*) was a French carol written in 1847 by Placide Cappeau de Roquemaure (1808–1877) at the request of the parish priest of Roquemaure in France. The tune was composed by Adolphe Charles Adams (1803–1856) that same year. American John Sullivan Dwight (1813–1893), a Unitarian minister, translated the song into English.

When it became widely known in France that the composer of "O Holy Night," Adolphe Charles Adams, was a Jew and that the lyricist, Placide Cappeau, had renounced his faith and become a Socialist, the Roman Catholic Church openly condemned the piece as being totally devoid of religious spirit. The Roman Catholic Church has since changed its stance on this carol. "O Holy Night" is traditionally sung in French churches at the stroke of midnight on Christmas Eve.

A well-known story states that in 1870, in trenches around the city of Paris, French and Prussian soldiers faced one another on Christmas Eve. All at once, they heard the voice of a French soldier singing "O Holy Night." When he was finished, a German soldier responded by singing Martin Luther's Christmas hymn "From Heaven Above to Earth I Come."

On December 24, 1906, several wireless radio operators picked up the sound of someone singing and speaking. They were tuned in to the first-ever radio broadcast. The man behind it was Canadian-born inventor Reginald Fessenden. The broadcast included Fessenden reciting the Christmas story and then playing "O Holy Night" on his violin. When it was over, he asked for anyone who had been able to hear the broadcast to contact him.

DID YOU KNOW?

Adolphe Charles Adams wrote numerous operas and ballets, including the celebrated *Giselle* (1841).

Once in Royal David's City

The lyrics of "Once in Royal David's City" were written in 1848 by Cecil Frances "Fanny" Alexander (1818–1895), wife of Ireland's Anglican primate. Her lyrics were set to a tune called "Irby" written in 1849 by Henry Gauntlett for this song.

Fanny Alexander was a Sunday school teacher who used music to teach children about the Christian religion. She wrote "Once in Royal David's City" after overhearing her godchildren complaining about how boring catechism was.

"Once in Royal David's City" was included in a book of hymns entitled *Hymns for Little Children* (1848) written by Fanny Alexander. It was one of 14 hymns designed to explain the various parts of the Apostles' Creed to children, in this case the third part of the Creed: "I believe in Jesus Christ who was conceived by the power of the Holy Ghost and born of the Virgin Mary." When the song first appeared in the hymn book, it was placed in the catechism section, not the Christmas section. The profits from *Hymns for Little Children* went to an institute for the deaf that Fanny Alexander founded at Strabane.

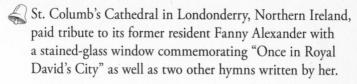 St. Columb's Cathedral in Londonderry, Northern Ireland, paid tribute to its former resident Fanny Alexander with a stained-glass window commemorating "Once in Royal David's City" as well as two other hymns written by her.

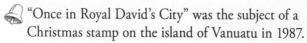 "Once in Royal David's City" was the subject of a Christmas stamp on the island of Vanuatu in 1987.

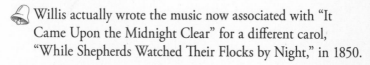 Mary Chapin Carpenter included "Once in Royal David's City" on her album *Come Darkness, Come Light: Twelve Songs of Christmas* (2008).

It Came Upon the Midnight Clear

"It Came Upon the Midnight Clear" was written in 1849 by Edmund Hamilton Sears (1810–1876), a Unitarian minister from Massachusetts. Sears wrote the hymn at the request of his minister friend William Parsons Lunt. It was first published in Boston's *Christian Register* on December 29, 1849. The song makes no mention of Jesus or the Nativity. The message of the song is "Peace on the earth, goodwill to men."

"It Came Upon the Midnight Clear" is set to different tunes in Great Britain and North America. Richard Storr Willis (1819–1900), a music critic and student of Mendelssohn, wrote the North American version called "Carol." The British version, known as "Noel," is a traditional tune adapted by Sir Arthur Sullivan (1842–1900).

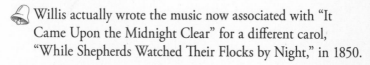 Willis actually wrote the music now associated with "It Came Upon the Midnight Clear" for a different carol, "While Shepherds Watched Their Flocks by Night," in 1850.

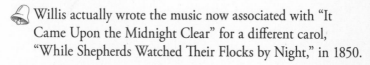 Methodist and Lutheran hymnals omit Sears' original third stanza, which speaks of sin and strife and war.

SONGS IN THE HYMNAL

🔔 Many artists have recorded versions of this song, including Frank Sinatra, Hall & Oates and Josh Groban. The 1997 *A Funky Little Christmas* compilation CD featured a surfer version of "It Came Upon the Midnight Clear."

🔔 The hymn has also been heard in several movies including *Melvin and Howard* (1980), *A Midnight Clear* (1992), *XX/XY* (2002), *Bad Santa* (2003) and *The Bad Harvest* (2005), and on a TV episode of *Grey's Anatomy*.

Good King Wenceslas

In 1582, Theodore Petri collected 74 songs into a compilation entitled *Devout Ecclesiastical and Scholastic Songs of the Old Bishops* for students at the cathedral school in Turku, Finland. It contained the medieval song *Tempus ad Floridum*. The English clergyman John Mason Neale wrote the carol "Good King Wenceslas" to go with this tune. It was first published in his 1853 collection, *Carols for Christmas-Tide*.

🔔 John Mason Neale also translated the medieval Latin carols "O Come, O Come, Emmanuel" (9th century) and "Good Christian Men, Rejoice" (14th century) into English.

🔔 "Good King Wenceslas" pertains not to Christmas Day but to St. Stephen's Day (December 26).

🔔 Britain produced a set of Christmas stamps in 1973 telling the story of Good King Wenceslas.

The Real Wenceslas

The man on whom the song was based lived in Bohemia during the 10th century. In Czech, the name Wenceslas is Vaclav. After his father died, Vaclav was raised by his Christian grandmother Ludmila. He was a duke who ruled his dukedom for only four years (925–929) before he was murdered by his pagan brother Boleslas on the steps of a church. He was canonized and is the patron saint of Bohemia. His skull is still crowned in special ceremonies at Prague's St. Vitus' Cathedral, a church founded by the duke himself.

While reputedly a kind ruler (though not a king), there is no basis for the tale told in the song. There is no equivalent carol in Czech.

Q: How does good King Wenceslas like his pizza?

A: Deep and crisp and even!

We Three Kings

When John Henry Hopkins Jr. wrote "We Three Kings" as a Christmas gift for his nieces and nephews in 1857, he was drawing on a long-standing tradition. In the Bible, the gospels mention magi coming to see the newborn Jesus and bringing him gifts. However, nowhere does it state how many magi came. Early Christian writers differ on the number, positing anywhere between two and 12 magi. Three was the number finally settled upon, probably because the Bible mentions three gifts that the Magi brought the Christ child—gold, frankincense and myrrh.

It is uncertain what the term *magi* (*magus* singular) means. Some translate it as "wise men" or "magicians." Most historians believe it refers to the astrologer priests of Zoroastrianism. Those people who say the word is another term for "king" draw upon the prophecy in Psalm 72:10: "The kings of Tarshish and the isles shall bring gifts; the kings of Sheba and Seba shall offer gifts."

The earliest names assigned to the three Magi were Bithisarea, Melchior and Gaspar in an anonymous Alexandrian manuscript from the early 6th century. In the West, these names evolved into Balthazar of Ethiopia, whose gift of frankincense alluded to the infant's role as a religious leader; Melchior of Arabia, whose gift of gold signified the child's role as a ruler; and Casper of Tarsus, whose gift of myrrh symbolized the babe's role as a healer.

By the 8th century, the ages of the Magi had been established. Balthazar was a young man, Casper was middle-aged and Melchior was elderly. By the 15th century, Casper was being depicted as black because medieval theologians concluded that each Magus must represent one of the three then-known races of man as descended from the three sons of Noah.

DID YOU KNOW?

King Henry VII of England (r. 1485–1509) offered packets of gold, frankincense and myrrh in the Royal Chapel at Christmas. This custom of the English monarch giving offerings of gold, frankincense and myrrh to the Church on Epiphany continues to the present day.

Kingly Caroling
The widespread nature of this tradition of three kings can be seen in the caroling customs from across Europe. In Germany and Belgium, groups of three men dressed as the three kings go singing from house to house on January 6, Ephiphany, the twelfth day of Christmas. They often receive gifts of food in return.

On Christmas Eve in France, Belgium and Hungary, three boys (girls in Hungary) were chosen by the local priest to dress as the three Magi and lead the other children through the town singing carols until they arrived at the church in time for Midnight Mass.

An earlier custom in Sweden was for three men dressed as kings, called the Star Boys, to go about singing carols. They followed another man carrying a light, the Star of Bethlehem, on a pole.

They were accompanied by two more men dressed as Herod and Judas who carried between them a bag in which to collect the coins given to the singers for their efforts. This custom died out in the 18th century.

At Santo Domingo, New Mexico, the Pueblo Indians celebrate Epiphany or Kings' Day with singing, dancing and gift-giving. A group of singers goes to the homes of officials and those whose surname is Rey or Reyes (i.e., King or Kings). There, they serenade the inhabitants until the homeowner goes onto the roof and throws presents down to the singers and the crowd of observers. The group then proceeds to the next house. This goes on all afternoon. The evening is filled with dancing.

DID YOU KNOW?

In the Argentinian folk carol "The Kings Arrived" (*Llegaron ya los Reyes*), the Wise Men bring syrup, honey and a poncho made from white alpaca wool.

Star of Wonder

"We Three Kings" refers to the "star of wonder, star of night / star of royal beauty bright" that guided the three Magi on their quest to find the birthplace of "the king of men." Known as the Star of Bethlehem, this bright light in the night sky is mentioned in the Gospel of Matthew. For centuries, scientists have tried to determine the exact year (and even date) of Jesus' birth by discovering which astronomical event was being referred to in Scriptures. A few different possibilities have been suggested, including the following ones.

In 7 BCE, Venus, Jupiter and Mars all appeared together near the moon, creating an extraordinarily bright light in the sky.

A lunar eclipse of Jupiter on April 17, 6 BCE, has been put forward as the "star" seen by the Wise Men.

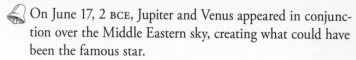

Chinese astronomers recorded a comet that appeared in 5 BCE that may have been the star followed by the Magi.

On June 17, 2 BCE, Jupiter and Venus appeared in conjunction over the Middle Eastern sky, creating what could have been the famous star.

DID YOU KNOW?

In Poland, Christmas is commonly referred to as *Gwiazdka* or "Little Star."

Other "Star"-ry Songs

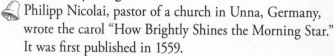

Philipp Nicolai, pastor of a church in Unna, Germany, wrote the carol "How Brightly Shines the Morning Star." It was first published in 1559.

In 1958, Tennessee Ernie Ford recorded "The Star Carol."

Both the words and music of "Every Star Shall Sing a Carol" were composed by Sydney Carter in 1961.

What Child Is This?

"What Child Is This?" was written in 1865 by William Chatterton Dix (1837–1898). He originally called it "The Manger Throne." The song was first published in *Christmas Carols New and Old* (1871), edited by Sir John Stainer and Reverend H.R. Bramley. "What Child Is This?" is popular in North America but is rarely heard in England anymore.

William Chatterton Dix was the general manager of a marine insurance company in Bristol. He was given the middle name of Chatterton in honor of the poet Thomas Chatterton, of whom Dix's father had written a biography.

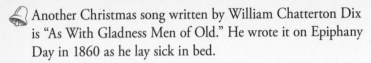 Another Christmas song written by William Chatterton Dix is "As With Gladness Men of Old." He wrote it on Epiphany Day in 1860 as he lay sick in bed.

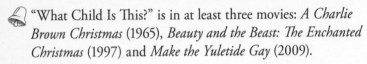 "What Child Is This?" is in at least three movies: *A Charlie Brown Christmas* (1965), *Beauty and the Beast: The Enchanted Christmas* (1997) and *Make the Yuletide Gay* (2009).

Greensleeves

Sir John Stainer first set Dix's lyrics to the tune of "Greensleeves," which dates back to at least the 16th century in England, when it appeared in print several times.

Since it was composed, the tune has been popular. Many lyrics have been set to it besides Dix's carol. The Cavaliers of the Royalist Party used it for a song supporting their cause during the English Civil War. In *The Beggar's Opera*, a prison lament is sung to it by Macheath. The song "Home in the Meadow" used the tune in the 1962 movie *How The West Was Won*. In the 1968 movie *Stay Away, Joe*, Elvis Presley sang "Stay Away" to it.

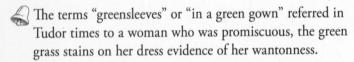 The terms "greensleeves" or "in a green gown" referred in Tudor times to a woman who was promiscuous, the green grass stains on her dress evidence of her wantonness.

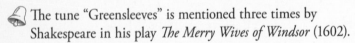 The tune "Greensleeves" is mentioned three times by Shakespeare in his play *The Merry Wives of Windsor* (1602).

O Little Town of Bethlehem

Phillips Brooks (1835–1893) wrote "O Little Town of Bethlehem" on Christmas Eve, 1868, for a Sunday school chorus to sing the following day. It was first performed at Holy Trinity Church in Philadephia, where Brooks was the rector. Brooks claimed he was inspired to write "O Little Town of Bethlehem" by a solitary horse ride from Jerusalem to Bethlehem, which he had undertaken on Christmas Eve, 1865.

Lewis Redner (1831–1908), who composed the original music for "O Little Town of Bethlehem," claimed the inspiration for the tune was brought to him by angels in a dream. Redner was the organist at Philadelphia's Holy Trinity Church.

"O Little Town of Bethlehem" is sung to different melodies in Great Britain and North America. In North America, the original tune written for it by Lewis Redner and entitled "St. Louis" is the most commonly heard, while the British prefer the traditional "Forest Green" as adapted by Ralph Vaughan Williams (1872–1958).

"Everywhere, Everywhere, Christmas Tonight" is another Christmas hymn written by Phillips Brooks with music by Lewis Redner.

"O Little Town of Bethlehem" was the favorite Christmas carol of Ulysses S. Grant (1822–1885), the Civil War general and later American president.

On Christmas Eve, a multi-denominational Protestant carol service is held in the field outside Bethlehem where it is claimed angels appeared to a group of shepherds, announcing Jesus' birth.

DID YOU KNOW?

Bethlehem, located in a fertile area of Israel five miles south of Jerusalem, means "house of bread." Besides the original Bethlehem, there are towns of that name in Wales, New Zealand and South Africa, as well as the American states of Maryland, Georgia, Kentucky and Indiana.

MORE SPIRITUAL SONGS

Christmas Carols for the Cradle

Not surprisingly, a holiday that revolves around the birth of
a baby has always included many lullabies in its musical repertoire. There were the previously mentioned medieval lullabies
(see p. 29), as well as the following popular carols.

Away in a Manger

"Away in a Manger" is an example of a modern lullaby or cradlesong. It is not known who wrote the lyrics for this carol. The
first two verses were first published in 1885 in an American
Lutheran hymn book. The third verse of "Away in a Manger"
was added in the early 20th century by John T. McFarland,
a Methodist minister.

The tune of "Away in a Manger" is different in Great Britain
than in North America. The British tune is "Cradlesong" by
William J. Kirkpatrick. The North American tune was written
by James R. Murray. The carol has been set to over 40 tunes over
the years.

Sleep, My Little Jesus

"Sleep, My Little Jesus" was written by William C. Gannett
(1840–1923), a Unitarian minister in Rochester, New York. The
music was composed by Adam Geibel, a blind composer. He was
born with sight but developed an eye infection at age eight or
nine. The doctor gave him too much medicine and he was left
blind. Nonetheless, he served as organist at Stetson Mission in
Philadelphia as an adult.

A Christmas Lullaby

On his 1990 album *On Praying Ground*, bluegrass musician
Arthel Lane "Doc" Watson included the song "A Christmas
Lullaby." The lyrics were adapted from the first three stanzas of

Isaac Watts' much longer hymn, "A Cradle Hymn." Doc Watson sings and composes music and also plays the guitar and banjo. The blind musician from North Carolina lost his sight to a childhood illness.

Ring Those Bells!

Church bells have a long association with all Christian celebrations, including Christmas and its associated feast days. In many areas of Europe, bells rang out on December 6, the Feast of St. Nicholas, to announce the arrival of that saintly man with his Christmas treats. In England, the beginning of the Christmas season fell on December 21, the Feast of St. Thomas, and the bells in the church towers could be heard ringing up to half a mile distant to welcome in the holiday.

An old legend dating back to at least the Middle Ages holds that bells rang out from the churches when Jesus was born. Another traditional tale is that the Devil died on Christmas Eve. Church bells were rung in a solemn toll for an hour before midnight in memory of this alleged event. Then the tune would change to a joyous peal to proclaim the birth of Our Lord.

This association of bells with Christmas still continues. Several Christmas songs recall the sounds of these merry instruments and the wondrous event that they announced.

Jingle Bells

James Pierpont (1822–1893) was asked by his father, a Unitarian minister in Medford, Massachusetts, to compose a song for the Thanksgiving service of 1857. The result was "Jingle Bells." People liked it so much that it was performed again at Christmas—and thereafter became a Christmas favorite in the region and beyond.

"Jingle Bells" was originally entitled "One Horse Open Sleigh." The original "Jingle Bells" had four verses and a chorus, but the last three verses are no longer sung.

"Jingle Bells" is the first Christmas song ever to have been recorded onto an album. The Hayden Quartet recorded it in 1902.

In 1965, Booker T and the MGs released a soul version of "Jingle Bells."

The first Christmas carol broadcast in space was "Jingle Bells" during the flight of *Gemini* VI in 1965. Astronauts Tom Stafford and Wally Schirra sang the carol to the accompaniment of a harmonica and sleigh bells.

The most frequently heard holiday song in films is "Jingle Bells." The list of movies in which it can be heard is long and includes *Jingle All the Way* (1996), *The Family Man* (2000), *Martian Child* (2007), *The Santa Clause* (1994), *Obsessed* (2009), *The Blind Side* (2009), *Driving Miss Daisy* (1989), *Friends with Money* (2006), *Bad Santa* (2003), *The Badge* (2002), *Crash* (1996/2004), *Dead Presidents* (1995), *Deuces Wild* (2002), *The Jacket* (2005), *L.A. Confidential* (1997), *Long Kiss Goodnight* (1996), *National Lampoon's Dorm Daze* (2003), *Raising Helen* (2004), *Reindeer Games* (2000), *Saved!* (2004), *Babe* (1995), *A Charlie Brown Christmas* (1965) and *Serving Sara* (2002).

I Heard the Bells on Christmas Day

Henry Wadsworth Longfellow (1807–1882) wrote the poem
"I Heard the Bells on Christmas Day" as an anti-war piece during the American Civil War after receiving news that his Union
soldier son had been wounded. The original verses four and five
are omitted today because they refer to the war:

> *Then from each black accursed mouth*
> *The cannon thundered in the South,*
> *And with the sound*
> *The carols drowned*
> *Of peace on earth, good will to men.*
>
> *It was as if an earthquake rent*
> *The hearth-stones of a continent,*
> *And made forlorn*
> *The households born*
> *Of peace on earth, good will to men.*

In 1872, the Englishman John Baptiste Calkin (1827–1905) set
Longfellow's poem to music.

Ding, Dong, Merrily on High

"Ding, Dong, Merrily on High" was written in 1924 by George
Ratcliffe Woodward, an English minister. The tune to which it is
now sung first appeared in 1589 in a book of French dances.

The tune of "Ding, Dong, Merrily on High" was that of a new
style of dance in 16th-century France. It was called the "branle"
and was danced with little springs, the men lifting the women
into the air by the waist.

Carol of the Bells

In 1936, Peter J. Wilhousky wrote some lyrics to go with a 1916
melody by Ukrainian Mykola D. Leontovich. The result was
"Carol of the Bells."

DID YOU KNOW?

John F. Kennedy's favorite Christmas song was "Silver Bells."

Spirituals from the Old South

Toward the end of the 19th century and into the 20th century, folklorists in the U.S. gathered the traditional songs sung by former African American slaves and poor people of the southern states. Chief amongst these collectors were John Wesley Work II (died 1925) and John Jacob Niles (1892–1980). Among the tunes they collected were some Christmas songs, some written in America and others brought over from England. Two of the ones that have become well known are "Go Tell It on the Mountain" and "I Wonder as I Wander."

Go Tell It on the Mountain

"Go Tell It on the Mountain" is a traditional African American folk carol. In the early 20th century, John Wesley Work II and his brother Frederick (1880–1942) re-did the traditional tune of the song to make it suitable for a choir to sing. There are innumerable versions of "Go Tell It on the Mountain."

I Wonder as I Wander

John Jacob Niles spent his life collecting and recording folk songs for posterity. In 1933, he heard a young girl named Annie Morgan singing "I Wonder as I Wander." The Morgan family was a poor but religious family who were holding a revival meeting in Murphy, North Carolina, to raise money for themselves. The girl told Niles that she had been taught the song by her mother, who had learned it from her own mother.

Niles paid Annie Morgan a quarter to sing the song slowly so he could write down the words. He was able to get three lines. The remainder he wrote himself, and "I Wonder as I Wander" was first published in Niles' collection of Southern spirituals entitled *Songs for the Hill-Folk: Twelve Ballads from Kentucky, Virginia, and North Carolina* (1934).

Carols by Christina

Several poems written by Christina Georgina Rossetti (1830–1894) have either been turned into Christmas hymns or served as the inspiration for holiday music. Christina Rossetti was the daughter of Gabriele Rossetti, an Italian exile to England, and Frances Polidori, herself the daughter of another Italian exile to England. Christina came from a family of writers and artists. Her maternal grandfather translated several English classics into Italian as well as writing some works of his own. Her father was a poet who expressed his political views in his poems. This first won him the favor of Ferdinand I of Naples but later his disapproval, resulting in the poet being exiled. Christina's elder sister Maria wrote a work about Dante Alighieri. Her two brothers helped to co-found the group of artists known as the Pre-Raphaelite brotherhood. They were both writers and poets, as well. The more well known of the two, Dante Gabriel Rossetti, provided illustrations for Christina's poems. He also used her as a model for his painting—e.g. as Mary in "The Girlhood of Mary Virgin" and "Annunciation, Ecce Ancilla Domini."

Rossetti was a well-known poet during her lifetime, writing under the pen name Ellen Alleyne. She was home-schooled by her mother, whom she later helped to run a private school out of their home. Later, she volunteered at a home for former prostitutes. Rossetti was an extremely religious person, a staunch High-Church Anglican. Indeed, her religious conviction was so strong that she rejected two suitors on religious grounds. In the early 1870s, Rossetti was diagnosed with Graves disease, a thyroid condition that left her bedridden for most of the remainder of her life. Nonetheless, she continued to write until her death in 1894. Several of her poems were published posthumously.

"Love Came Down at Christmas" is one of Rossetti's poems to have been set to music. It was first sung to music written by Reginald Owen Morris in 1886. Later, Harold Darke (1888–1976) composed a different melody for it.

"In the Bleak Midwinter" was not published until 1904, a decade after her death. It was first set to music by Gustav Holst (1874–1934) two years later, at which time it was included in the English Hymnal. In 1909, Harold Darke composed a different arrangement for the poem, eliminating the fourth of the five verses. Since then, several other composers have set the poem to their own tunes.

More recently, Rossetti's poem "Christmas Eve" served as the inspiration for Tansy Davies' winning entry to the 2011 King's College-commissioned carol competition. Davies' work is entitled "Christmas Hath a Darkness."

Alfred Burt and the Christmas Card Carols

The Burt family of Pontiac, Michigan, was a very religious family. Father Bates Burt was the minister at All Saints Church in Pontiac. The family was also quite musical, and in 1922, Bates Burt composed a Christmas song to write in the family's Christmas cards. It became an annual Burt family tradition.

Bates Burt wrote the lyrics and composed the music for the family Christmas card songs until 1941, when he invited his son Alfred (1920–1954), a trumpet player, to compose the music. When Bates died of a heart attack in 1948, a new lyricist was found in the person of Wihla Hutson (1901–2002), the long-time organist at All Saints Church and a close family friend. Alfred Burt and Hutson continued to write Christmas songs together until Burt passed away from lung cancer in 1954. He finished composing the music to his last song, "The Star Carol," less than 24 hours before he died. Later that year, 12 of Burt's carols were released on the album *The Christmas Mood*.

It was not until a few years later that Hutson decided to continue on her own. In 1982, 18 of Hutson's own carols were published.

The Burt family Christmas card carols were revived in 2001 when Abbie Betinis, a grandniece of Alfred Burt and a composer herself, began to include songs she had written in her cards.

- In 1948, Alfred Burt composed a tune to accompany "Christ in a Strangers' Guise," an old text supplied to him by his brother John, a minister.

- "Sleep, Baby Mine" was written in 1949 to announce the birth of Alfred and Anne Burt's daughter Diane.

- The 1951 carol "Some Children See Him" was meant as a unifying song for people whose lives over the past decade had been torn apart by wars—first, World War II and then, the Korean War. In 1995, the government of Palau issued a series of stamps commemorating this carol.

Nat King Cole recorded the Burt-Hutson 1954 song "Caroling, Caroling" in 1960.

In 1967, Simon and Garfunkel released their version of the Burt-Hutson song "The Star Carol."

Kenny Loggins recorded "Christmas Cometh Caroling," the first carol on which Alfred Burt had collaborated with his father Bates.

The other carols co-written by the Burt father and son team are "Jesu Parvule" (1943), "What Are the Signs" (1944), "Ah, Bleak and Chill the Wintry Wind" (1945), "All on a Christmas Morning" (1946) and "Nigh Bethlehem" (1947).

Further Burt-Hutson Christmas carols are "This is Christmas" (or "Bright, Bright, the Holly Berries") (1950), "Come, Dear Children" (1952), "O Hearken Ye" (1953) and "We'll Dress the House" (1954).

The Little Drummer Boy

"The Little Drummer Boy" is one of a variety of Christmas folk-tales that revolves around a poor child who is a witness to Jesus' birth but has nothing to give the newborn baby. In some versions, such as the Mexican tale of a little girl, a miracle occurs and the child finds him- or herself in the possession of a gift— poinsettias in the Mexican story. In other versions, such as the song "The Little Drummer Boy," the child offers the Christ Child something non-material, in this case his talent for playing the drums.

The original lyrics of "The Little Drummer Boy" were written in 1941 by Katherine Kennicott Davis (1892–1980). She titled the piece "Carol of the Drum." It is the slightly revised lyrics that made it a hit in 1959.

Katherine Davis bequeathed her royalties from "The Little Drummer Boy" to the music program at her alma mater, Wellesley College.

Bing Crosby originally rejected "The Little Drummer Boy." However, by the end of his career, the song was so popular that he reversed his earlier decision. It was the last Christmas song he ever recorded.

"The Little Drummer Boy" inspired an animated movie of the same name starring Greer Garson. It first aired in 1968.

President Richard Nixon's favorite Christmas song was "The Little Drummer Boy."

Hard rock versions of "The Little Drummer Boy" were made by Jimi Hendrix, Joan Jett and Bob Seger and the Silver Bullet Band.

In 1985, Cameroun released a Christmas stamp showing the Nativity scene and the little drummer boy.

DID YOU KNOW?

The French carol "Patapan" was written by Bernard de la Monnoye (1641–1728) and published in 1720 in a booklet entitled *Burgundian Noëls*. The song is a precursor of "The Little Drummer Boy."

The Legend of the Christmas Rose

People in the medieval period had an abundance of stories, often religious in nature, that explained the existence of many natural phenomena. This is true about some small white flowers (*Helleborus niger*) that bloom during the cold winter months. They are known as Christmas roses.

According to the medieval legend, a poor young girl named Madelon wished to go and see the infant Jesus. She was afraid to do so, however, because she was ashamed at having nothing to give the Babe while others were taking him gifts of gold, frankincense and myrrh. Overcome with despair, Madelon sat in a field and cried. An angel spotted the sad girl and caused beautiful white flowers to spring from the ground made wet by her tears. Happily surprised, Madelon quickly gathered a bouquet of the blooms and went to present them to the Holy Infant, who loved them as much as the more costly gifts bestowed upon him by the Magi.

It became customary in some regions of Europe to grow the plant near the entrance to one's house. This ensured that every year, there would be Christmas roses waiting as gifts for Jesus on the day of the celebration of his birth. They were a sign that he was welcome in the home.

Thomas Dunhill (1877–1946) composed a Christmas cantata in 1933. It was called *Cantata of the Nativity (The Christmas Rose)*.

"Christmas Roses," written by Paula Frances and N.A. Catsos in 1953, was first recorded by Hank Snow (1914–1999) in 1967 on his album *Christmas with Hank Snow*. In 1987, Canadian musician William T. "Paddy" Gearin (1936–2007) recorded a version for his holiday album, *A Newfoundland Christmas*. The lyrics speak of a man sending Christmas roses to his lover at Christmas because he is unable to be with her in person.

In 1989, George Jones recorded a version of this story in his song "The Legend of the Christmas Rose." It was released on the *Lonely Christmas Call* album, a compilation of holiday songs by various artists.

Kings and Shepherds

Appointed Queen's Master of Music in 2004, Sir Peter Maxwell Davies put his talents to work in 2007 to write a new Christmas carol for Queen Elizabeth II's enjoyment. The song, "Kings and Shepherds," is based on a poem written by his good friend, the late Orcadian poet Sir George Mackay Brown (1921–1996), called "Hamnavoe Women and the Wareth Bell: Midwinter." This poem and the carol honor Christmas as it is celebrated in the remote Scottish Orkney Islands, home of Davies and Brown. Brown's poem is a favorite of many, and portions of it have been used in Christmas cards.

Davies is a composer who works in a wide variety of genres—ballet, opera, choral works and chamber music. He is the first Queen's Master of Music to have been appointed for 10 years rather than the traditional life term. This limited term will enable more deserving musicians to hold the post.

Carols at Court
Singing has always had a place at court, especially on festive occasions such as holiday celebrations.

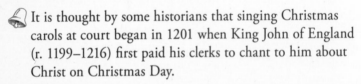 It is thought by some historians that singing Christmas carols at court began in 1201 when King John of England (r. 1199–1216) first paid his clerks to chant to him about Christ on Christmas Day.

William Dunbar wrote Christmas carols for the court of King James IV of Scotland (r. 1488–1513).

Every Twelfth Day, Elizabeth I (r. 1568–1603) hosted a masque at court. It was kicked off with a carol sung by the Children of the Royal Chapel.

The composer Robert Herrick (1591–1674) wrote carols for the Chapel Royal at Whitehall.

SOME SECULAR SONGS

Winter Wonderland

Dick Smith was a 33-year-old songwriter dying of tuberculosis when he wrote "Winter Wonderland" one winter day in 1934 after watching a group of children playing in the snow from a window in the sanatorium. It was his biggest hit. The song was recorded that same year by Guy Lombardo and the Royal Canadians. Aretha Franklin released a pop version in 1964.

The happy, upbeat "Winter Wonderland," which celebrates so many of the sights, sounds and activities of the season, has been used in several films, including *When Harry Met Sally* (1989), *Rover Dangerfield* (1991), *Rocky V* (1990), *Elf* (2003), *Better Off Dead* (1985), *Bad Santa* (2003), *Assault on Precinct 13* (2005), *Fast Times at Ridgemont High* (1982), *While You Were Sleeping* (1995), *The Holiday* (2006), *Michael* (1996), *Eloise at Christmastime* (2003) and *Polar Express* (2004).

White Christmas

Not only is it the best song I ever wrote, it's the best song anybody ever wrote.

–Irving Berlin

Without a doubt, Irving Berlin's "White Christmas" is one of the most popular Christmas songs ever written. It is definitely the most recorded, with over 500 versions. It has been recorded in a variety of musical styles, including rock-and-roll (e.g., Elvis Presley), doo-wop (e.g., The Drifters), jazz (e.g., Charles Parker) and reggae (e.g., Bob Marley). The version recorded by Bing Crosby has sold 31 million copies alone.

Berlin wrote an opening verse to "White Christmas," which he later omitted. It spoke of being in sunny Los Angeles at Christmastime but longing for the wintry north. When Berlin deleted the opening verse to "White Christmas," he transformed the song, forcing the singer or listener to provide the context for the lyrics. This is likely what makes it so appealing.

🔔 Walter Scharf worked with Berlin, who could not read musical notation, to add the orchestration to "White Christmas."

🔔 The first public performance of "White Christmas" was given by Bing Crosby on the Kraft Music Hall radio broadcast on Christmas Eve, 1941.

🔔 When Bing Crosby's rendition of "White Christmas" appeared on the Hit Parade countdown on October 17, 1942, at number seven, it was the first time a Christmas song had ever charted in the weekly survey. It went on to become the number one song of 1942. In 1944, 1946, 1947 and 1969, it was the number one Christmas song.

🔔 "White Christmas" won an Oscar for best song in 1942.

🔔 Apparently, "White Christmas" was considered primarily a love song by young people when it was first released.

The Ravens recorded a rhythm-and-blues version in 1948. Cowboy Copas recorded a country version that same year.

The only recording of "White Christmas" that includes Irving Berlin's original first verse is Darlene Love's 1963 version.

Irving Berlin tried unsuccessfully to get Elvis Presley's recording of "White Christmas" banned by radio stations. Berlin considered Presley's rendition to be vulgar and irreverent.

"White Christmas" was introduced in the movie *Holiday Inn* in 1942. Since then, it has been used in numerous other films, such as *Polar Express* (2004), *The Santa Clause 3: The Escape Clause* (2006), *Home Alone* (1990), *Four Christmases* (2008), *The Santa Clause* (1994), *Love Actually* (2003) and *Miracle* (2004).

DID YOU KNOW?

There have been only 14 white Christmases in New York City since 1912.

Holiday Inn

Irving Berlin's "White Christmas" was featured in the 1942 musical comedy *Holiday Inn*. In this movie, Jim Hardy (Bing Crosby) and Ted Hanover (Fred Astaire) are a song-and-dance duo. Jim decides to quit the hectic life of the city and retire to a country inn, but not before his partner steals his girlfriend, Lila (Virginia Dale). Later, Jim decides to produce a Christmas show at his inn and falls for Linda (Marjorie Reynolds), one of the women in his production. However, once again, Ted appears on the scene and steals Jim's lady with promises of stardom. Jim pursues the pair back to Hollywood, where he woos Linda back.

🔔 Berlin would only agree to a contract with Paramount Pictures to do *Holiday Inn* if Bing Crosby was given the lead role.

🔔 "White Christmas" is sung twice in *Holiday Inn*. The first time it is performed as a loving duet by Linda and Jim at the inn. The second time is at the end of the movie when Linda chooses love over success in her career.

🔔 Actress Marjorie Reynolds lip-synchs "White Christmas" with Crosby in *Holiday Inn*; it is actually the voice of Martha Mears that one hears.

DID YOU KNOW?

Irving Berlin's "White Christmas" was featured in another movie in 1954. The movie was named *White Christmas* after the song and in hopes of attracting viewers.

White Christmas and the War

"White Christmas" became such a big hit partly because of when it was released. The United States and much of the world was embroiled in World War II. Soldiers and civilians alike were sick and tired of the fighting and wanted it to end so they could go on with their lives. Soldiers away from their families longed to return home, especially during traditional family gathering times such as the Christmas holidays. The lyrics of "White Christmas" struck a chord with many as they articulated the desire for things to go back to the way they were before the war. The song also reminded the soldiers of the lifestyle and values that they were fighting to defend.

While Christmas carols were popular anthems of World War II in the West, the same was not true in Germany. Indeed, the Nazi government looked upon anyone caught singing Christmas carols with grave suspicion as it indicated an allegiance to something other than the Party.

DID YOU KNOW?

The U.S. Army's 99th Infantry Division banned the singing or humming of "White Christmas" during the Christmas season of 1944 so that the soldiers in their precarious foxhole positions in the German-Belgian forests would be able to remain focused.

Irving Berlin: Songwriter Extraordinaire

Irving Berlin, composer of some 3000 songs, was one of the most prolific songwriters ever. While many people know that Berlin wrote "White Christmas," here is a list of other facts about the man that most do not know.

- Irving Berlin was born Israel (Izzy) Baline in Siberia in 1888.

- He quit school at the age of 12. At 13, he ran away from home and began living on the streets.

- This writer of the hit Christmas song "White Christmas" was Jewish.

- He was self-taught in music, having received no instruction in either songwriting or piano playing. Indeed, Berlin could not even read music.

- Irving Berlin and his wife Ellin Mackay Berlin dreaded the holiday season ever since their three-week-old son Irving Jr. died on Christmas Day in 1928.

He was awarded the U.S. Army's Medal of Merit in 1945 and the Congressional Gold Medal in 1954 for his patriotic songwriting.

In 1963, he received a special Tony Award for his many contributions to American musicals.

He was presented with a Grammy in 1968 for his lifetime achievements.

Irving Berlin has a star on the Hollywood Walk of Fame. It was unveiled in 1994.

"White Christmas" ended up being Berlin's second favorite composition. His favorite was "God Bless America." Some of his other hit songs are "Alexander's Ragtime Band," "Blue Skies," "Cheek to Cheek," "Puttin' On the Ritz," "Say It Isn't So" and "There's No Business Like Show Business."

Irving Berlin died in 1989—he lived to be 101 years old.

DID YOU KNOW?

Between 1967 and 1989, singer and composer John Wallowich and friends gathered once a year outside 17 Beekman Place in New York City, home of composer Irving Berlin, to sing "White Christmas."

I'll Be Home for Christmas

Lyricists Buck Ram and Kim Gannon, along with composer Walter Kent, wrote the popular holiday song "I'll Be Home for Christmas" in 1943 to cash in on people's desire to be reunited during the war. Irving Berlin's "White Christmas," released a year earlier, had done very well.

🔔 Bing Crosby's recording of this song sold over one million copies.

🔔 When the *Gemini* VII space shuttle was returning to earth on December 17, 1965, after having completed 206 orbits of the earth, astronauts James Lovell and Frank Borman requested to hear the song "I'll Be Home for Christmas" as recorded by Bing Crosby.

🔔 Oscar Petersen performed this song on the soundtrack for the 2007 movie *This Christmas*.

Q: What is Sherlock's favorite Christmas song?

A: I'll be Holmes for Christmas.

Bing Crosby, the Christmas Crooner
Bing Crosby (1903–1977) is one of the most successful singers in history. Three hundred and ninety-six songs recorded by Crosby made the music charts, with 38 reaching number one—that's 14 more number one hit songs than The Beatles. Crosby, nicknamed "Santa Cros," popularized many Christmas songs, both traditional and new. His most successful Christmas recording was "White Christmas" (1942) by Irving Berlin. It was number one on the Hit Parade for a record of 10 consecutive weeks. The song struck a chord with the many soldiers and civilians whose lives had been disrupted by World War II.

🔔 In 1935, Bing Crosby's first Christmas radio broadcast was heard.

In 1942 and 1943, Bing Crosby had the number one Christmas hits—"White Christmas" and "I'll Be Home for Christmas," respectively.

Crosby's rendition of "White Christmas" made the Hit Parade every December between 1942 and 1961, except 1953.

Crosby sang "White Christmas" in three movies—*Holiday Inn* (1942), *Blue Skies* (1946) and *White Christmas* (1954).

Bing Crosby's *Merry Christmas* LP (1945), a collection of Christmas songs, was the first such collection and the best-selling record ever before the invention of CDs.

He sang "Silent Night" in the 1945 movie *The Bells of St. Mary.*

Crosby first recorded "A Marshmallow World" in 1949. That same year, he rejected the song "Rudolph, the Red-Nosed Reindeer."

In 1962, Bing Crosby presented his first Christmas special on television.

Crosby's last television recording was in 1977 when he and rock musician David Bowie sang a duet of "The Little Drummer Boy."

Bing Crosby was a devout Catholic who had even contemplated becoming a priest in his younger years. He did not feel right about making money from recordings of religious songs and donated his income from recordings of religious Christmas carols to an American Catholic Mission in China.

The Christmas Song

On a very hot July day in 1944, songwriters Mel Torme and Robert Wells were in Toluca, California, thinking of ways to help them stay cool. They decided to write a Christmas song. The result was "The Christmas Song (Chestnuts Roasting on an Open Fire)." It took them only 45 minutes to write.

The King Cole Trio, led by singer Nat King Cole, was the first to record the song in 1946. Their rendition is still the most popular one and is the most frequently played Christmas song on American radio.

"The Christmas Song" has been played in several movies, including *The Santa Clause 3: The Escape Clause* (2006), *Jingle All the Way* (1996), *Scrooged* (1988), *Obsessed* (2009), *The Girl Next Door* (2004), *Catch Me If You Can* (2002), *Dickie Roberts: Former Child Star* (2003) and *The Rookie* (2002).

The term "Jack Frost," as in the lyric "Jack Frost nipping at your nose," is derived from the Norse *Jakul Frosti*, meaning "icicle frost."

Let It Snow!

After a busy day at work in July 1945, musician Jule Styne and lyricist Sammy Cahn wanted to cool off. Cahn also wanted to relax and suggested a drive to one of Los Angeles' beaches for a swim. Styne, however, wished to continue working and suggested writing a song about winter. The result was "Let It Snow! Let It Snow! Let It Snow!"

Vaughn Monroe recorded "Let It Snow! Let It Snow! Let It Snow!" on October 31, 1945, and took it to number one on the charts. The song seemed to be a particularly apt way for Americans to greet the first peaceful Christmas after years of war during which the tune "White Christmas" had spurred them on. Years later, in 1997, the holiday CD *A Funky Little Christmas* included the reggae song "Latin Snow, Latin Snow, Let It Snow."

Snow and Christmas

Snow seems to be something that people the world over associate with Christmas, whether or not there is actually snow in their area at that time of the year. In Canada, it is not often that people see a Christmas without any snow on the ground. Nonetheless, it has been a goal of retailers and manufacturers since the late 19th century to come up with a safe and profitable method to bring the celebrated white stuff inside for the holidays. Here are a number of things they have tried:

 Glass flakes (1882)

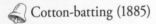 Cotton-batting (1885)

Powdered ammonia (early 20th century)

Borax flakes (early 20th century)

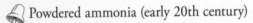 Popcorn (early 20th century)

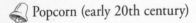 Mica or diamond dust (1903)

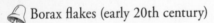 Mica and asbestos mixture (1928)

In more recent years, people have used stearic acid made from cow carcasses and dispensed from aerosol cans, as well as plastic snow and tinsel.

Sleigh Ride

Composer Leroy Anderson got the idea for his hit tune "Sleigh Ride" while on summer vacation in 1946. It took two years for him to complete. The instrumental version of the song was first recorded in 1949 by Arthur Fiedler and the Boston Pops. The following year, in 1950, Mitchell Parish wrote lyrics to go with the music.

🔔 In the song, a sleigh ride is compared to a print by Currier & Ives, a popular 19th-century printing company that closed in 1907. The original lyrics by Parish refer to a birthday party, not a Christmas party, even though some artists—such as The Carpenters and Air Supply—changed this. Actually, there is no mention of Christmas at all in the lyrics.

🔔 This song has been recorded by many artists in a variety of genres. In both 2010 and 2011, "Sleigh Ride" was the most-played holiday song on American radio.

Movies that have featured "Sleigh Ride" include *Jingle All the Way* (1996), *Jack Frost* (1998), *Home Alone 2: Lost in New York* (1992), *The Family Man* (2000), *Four Christmases* (2008), *Dirty Dancing: Havana Nights* (2004) and *Elf* (2003).

It's Beginning to Look a Lot Like Christmas

"It's Beginning to Look a Lot Like Christmas" was written by Meredith Willson (1902–1984). It was first recorded by Perry Como in 1951. It has also been recorded by Bing Crosby, Johnny Mathis and Michael Bublé.

The Hopalong boots for which the boy in the song wishes refer to the ones worn by the Hollywood character Hopalong Cassidy.

Meredith Willson also wrote the hit Broadway musical *The Music Man* (1957).

The song was used in the 1963 musical *Here's Love*, also by Meredith Willson.

Mathis' version of the song was featured in the 1992 movie *Home Alone 2: Lost in New York*.

In 2006, the British supermarket chain Asda used the song in its Christmas commercial.

(There's No Place Like) Home for the Holidays

In 1954, Al Stillman and Bob Allen co-wrote "(There's No Place Like) Home for the Holidays" for singer Perry Como. Allen wrote the music and Stillman the lyrics. Como recorded the song twice—in 1954 and 1959—the second time with a different musical accompaniment. The first recording is the better-known one.

 Some other singers who have recorded "(There's No Place Like) Home for the Holidays" include Garth Brooks, Randy Travis, Barry Manilow, Olivia Newton-John and The Carpenters.

 The song was included on the soundtrack for the 2008 movie *Four Christmases*.

 Cyndi Lauper and Norah Jones recorded it as a duet in 2011.

DID YOU 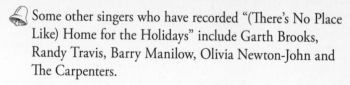 KNOW?

Jewish songwriter Phil Spector's song "Christmas (Baby Please Come Home)," recorded by Darlene Love, was released on November 22, 1963, the same day President John F. Kennedy was assassinated. Spector pulled the song and had Love record a new version that was released following the holidays—"Johnny Please Come Home."

Perry Como

Singer Perry Como (1912–2001) got a late start in the music industry as well as an unexpected one. Como had worked as a barber since the age of 13 and at the age of 20 had moved to Meadville, Pennsylvania, to work with his uncle. He attended a dance where Freddy Carlone was playing with his orchestra. Carlone invited people up to sing. Urged on by his buddies, Como went up. After hearing him sing, Carlone offered him a job.

Como traveled and sang in bands from 1932 until 1942, shortly after the birth of his first child. He returned to the music business in 1943 after being offered his own radio program, which meant he no longer had to travel. Later, he switched to television and even starred in some films. Every year, he sang "Ave Maria" on his television Christmas special but refused to perform it at concerts, stating it was not appropriate.

Como always placed his family above his musical career and refused to speak publicly about his private life. He and his wife, Roselle Belline Como, were married for 65 years until her death in 1998.

Como recorded many Christmas songs, both old and new, including "Christ is Born," "Christmas Bells (in the Steeple)," "Christmas Eve," "Christmas Dream," "The Christmas Symphony," "Have Yourself a Merry Little Christmas," "Jingle Bells," "The Little Drummer Boy," "Love is a Christmas Rose," "O Holy Night," "Silver Bells," "There is No Christmas Like a Home Christmas," "We Wish You a Merry Christmas," "White Christmas" and "Winter Wonderland."

Jingle Bell Rock

"Jingle Bell Rock" was co-authored by Joseph Beal and James R. Boothe. Bobby Helms' rendition of the song was the number one Christmas hit of 1957, reaching number one on the charts less than two weeks after it was released.

🔔 "Jingle Bell Rock" was the first song to blend the new rock-and-roll style of music with Christmas.

🔔 Bobby Rydell and Chubby Checker's rendition of "Jingle Bell Rock" was the number one Christmas song of 1961.

🔔 "Jingle Bell Rock" is an especially popular holiday song in the movies. You can hear it sung in several, including *Jingle All the Way* (1996), *Jack Frost* (1998), *Home Alone 2: Lost in New York* (1992), *Surviving Christmas* (2004), *Four Christmases* (2008), *Bad Santa* (2003), *Elf* (2003), *Gross Anatomy* (1989), *Lethal Weapon* (1987), *Mean Girls* (2004), *Trading Places* (1983) and *Vanilla Sky* (2001).

Rockin' Around the Christmas Tree

Brenda Lee recorded Johnny Marks' "Rockin' Around the Christmas Tree" in 1958 and got a number one Christmas hit. She was 13 years old when she recorded the song.

 Ronnie Spector and Darlene Love recorded the song for the charity album *A Very Special Christmas 2* (1992).

An instrumental version was played on the animated movie *Rudolph, the Red-Nosed Reindeer* (1964). It has also featured in several other films, including *Home Alone* (1990), *Jingle All the Way* (1996), *The Holiday* (2006), *Cheaper by the Dozen* (2003), *Long Kiss Goodnight* (1996), *Miracle* (2004) and *Reindeer Games* (2000).

Johnny Marks and St. Nicholas Music

Irving Berlin was not the only Jewish composer of Christmas songs. Indeed, many of the more well-known Christmas songs of the 20th century were written by Jewish songwriters, the most prolific of whom was Johnny Marks.

Johnny Marks specialized in Christmas tunes, naming his publishing company St. Nicholas Music. He is best known as the composer of "Rudolph, the Red-Nosed Reindeer" (see p. 123), a song that accounted for 75 percent of his income annually. His song "When Santa Claus Gets Your Letter" was inspired by the many letters to Santa received by the *New York Times* newspaper requesting Santa to bring copies of his "Rudolph, the Red-Nosed Reindeer" record for Christmas.

Other Christmas songs written by Johnny Marks include "A Merry, Merry Christmas to You," "Silver and Gold," "The Most Wonderful Day of the Year," "Jingle, Jingle, Jingle," "A Caroling We Go" and "A Holly Jolly Christmas." Marks also adapted Clement Moore's poem, "'Twas the Night Before Christmas," into a song and wrote music to go with it.

Both Johnny Marks and Irving Berlin were awarded the Spirit of Christmas Award in 1973 by the International Society of Santa Claus.

Other Christmas Songs by Jewish Songwriters

Jewish teenagers Mel Torme and Robert Wells wrote "The Christmas Song."

Walter Kent and Buck Ram, who co-wrote "I'll Be Home for Christmas," were both Jewish.

Mitchell Parrish, the man who wrote the lyrics for the popular holiday song "Sleigh Ride," was Jewish.

Put Your Dancing Shoes On

The word "carol" was originally used to mean a dance song. While this meaning died out sooner in areas where the Protestant Reformation took hold and dancing became equated with sin and temptation, in Catholic areas many Christmas songs continued to be danced to as well as sung. In 18th-century France, secular Christmas songs were often danced as gavottes or minuets. Many Polish carols are set to dance music such as the polonaise and the mazurka.

One English carol that has survived from the time when singing and dancing went together at Christmas festivities is "Tomorrow Shall Be My Dancing Day." The carol describes life as a dance much in the same manner as the modern song "Lord of the Dance," written by Sydney Carter in 1967.

By the middle of the 20th century, the notion of dancing to Christmas music was making a comeback. Several songs were introduced specifically for this purpose. Undoubtedly the best-known Christmas dance song is Johnny Marks' "Rockin' Around the Christmas Tree," but there have been others as well.

🔔 In 1949, "The Merry Christmas Polka" was written by Paul Francis Weber with music by Sonny Burke.

🔔 "The Christmas Waltz," with lyrics by Sammy Cahn and music by Jule Styne, was written in 1954 at the request of Frank Sinatra.

🔔 In 1961, Twistin' Kings put a seasonal spin on the newest dance craze with "Xmas Twist."

In the past few decades, a number of holiday songs have been set to a dance beat. Today, there are many songs from which to choose for those who feel like letting go and shaking their booty!

CAROLS ABOUT CHRISTMAS CHARACTERS

Santa Claus

The modern-day Santa Claus developed in the United States during the 19th century. Dutch colonists had brought with them Sinterklaas (or Saint Nicholas), who delivered treats to children on December 6, the feast day of Saint Nicholas. In 1823, Clement Moore (1779–1863) wrote a poem for his children called "'Twas the Night before Christmas" that caught the hearts and imaginations of many who read it. The German-American illustrator Thomas Nast (1840–1902) created the Santa Claus we are familiar with today in a series of drawings done over a period of 30 years.

Not surprisingly, several Christmas songs deal with that jolly old fellow in red. The earliest Christmas song about the then newly created character of Santa Claus was "Up on the Housetop." It was written by Benjamin Hanby (1833–1867) in 1864.

Santa Claus Is Coming to Town

The most successful Santa song is "Santa Claus Is Coming to Town." Haven Gillespie wrote the song on the back of an envelope while sitting in a bar in 1932. It took him 15 minutes. Fred Coots wrote the music to go with Gillespie's lyrics. It then took Gillespie and Coots two years to find a singer willing to record their song.

Eddie Cantor originally rejected singing "Santa Claus Is Coming to Town" because it was a "kiddie's song." His wife Ida eventually convinced him to sing it. When Cantor first played "Santa Claus Is Coming to Town" on his radio show, it became an instant hit. By morning, the station had received 100,000 letters requesting a copy of the sheet music.

🔔 Eddie Cantor sang "Santa Claus Is Coming to Town" in the Macy's Christmas parade of 1934.

🔔 The song was made into an animated movie in 1970.

🔔 "Santa Claus Is Coming to Town" is the third-best-selling Christmas song ever.

🔔 This song has been recorded by numerous artists. Celine Dion released a French version in 1981.

🔔 "Santa Claus Is Coming To Town" is heard in *The Godfather* (1972), *Polar Express* (2004), *Home Alone* (1990), *Scrooged* (1998), *Surviving Christmas* (2004), *Four Christmases* (2008), *The Santa Clause* (1994), *Simon Birch* (1998), *Elf* (2003) and *The Santa Clause 2* (2002).

🔔 The lyrics and title of the song were revised for the movie *Merry Madagascar* in 2009—"Santa Claus Is Coming to Madagascar."

Here Comes Santa Claus

Another well-known Christmas song about children's favorite holiday gift-giver is "Here Comes Santa Claus." Gene Autry, singer of many popular Christmas songs, not only sang "Here Comes Santa Claus" but also wrote it. Autry got the idea for the song when riding in the annual Hollywood Christmas Parade in 1946. All around him the children were shouting, "Here comes Santa Claus!" By the end of the parade, Autry had thought up the lyrics to the song.

 Oakley Haldeman composed the score for "Here Comes Santa Claus."

"Here Comes Santa Claus" was used in the 2007 Christmas movie *Fred Claus* starring Vince Vaughn and Paul Giamatti.

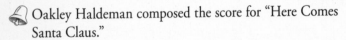

DID YOU KNOW?

In southern Nova Scotia (Acadia), residents used to practice a custom known as "Santy Clausing." Children would dress as Santa Claus and go from house to house singing and dancing during the twelve days of Christmas. They carried with them a bag to collect all the "santys" they received in return. Santys were usually cookies, cakes or candies.

Santa Claus, Indiana, USA

Abe Olman (1888–1984) and Al Jacobs (1903–1985) wrote the song "Santa Claus, Indiana, USA" in 1959. In this song, the singer wants to visit this community to retrieve all the letters that accidentally went there rather than to Santa Claus' real home at the North Pole. The singer wants to rectify the situation by sending these children the presents meant for the singer's own parents.

Thankfully, the singer need not worry. There is a group of local people in Santa Claus, Indiana, who get together every December to reply to the many letters addressed to Santa Claus the post office there receives. This group calls themselves Santa's Elves.

The post office in Santa Claus, Indiana, receives many Christmas cards and letters every year from people wanting them stamped with the town's postmark. Every year, the town selects a piece of artwork by a student at the local school to be made into a special postmark used only that December.

The town does much to encourage the tourist trade that its name attracts. The three lakes surrounding the community have holiday-themed names—Christmas Lake, Lake Holly and Lake Noël. All the streets in town have holiday-themed names. There are also numerous attractions and events for visitors.

While Santa Claus, Indiana, is the only town in the U.S. with a Christmas name to have a song written about it, it is only one of a group of "Christmas towns." There is a town in Georgia that is also named Santa Claus. It is much smaller than its Indiana counterpart. It too has carried the holiday-theme to some of its street names, including Rudolph Way, Dancer Street, Prancer Street, Sleigh Street and Candy Cane Lane.

Then there is a community in Alaska called North Pole. Its post office is also a popular place in December with people wanting their Christmas correspondence postmarked at the North Pole. At another North Pole—this one in Indiana—Santa has set up a workshop.

The United States is not the only place in the world where Santa Claus can be found. Children writing to Father Christmas in Great Britain have their letters processed at a depot near Belfast known as Reindeer Land.

Near Rovaniemi, the capital of Finland's Lapland, an area has been developed into a tourist center called Santa Claus Village. There is a post office that responds to children's letters to Santa. There are also reindeer to visit—and eat. Of course, people can also visit Santa Claus.

The Man in the Santa Suit
In 2005, the power pop group Fountains of Wayne released the song "The Man in the Santa Suit" on their album *Out-of-State Plates*. This song is about an unemployed man who takes a seasonal job as a department store Santa Claus, a position he finds humiliating.

Neil Halstead released a version of this song in 2011 on the compilation CD *This Warm December*.

The Development of Department Store Santas
The first department store Santa Claus in Canada appeared in G.A. Holland & Son in Montreal in 1899.

Some early-20th-century Americans worried that the growing number of street and store Santas might cause children to stop believing in Santa. In 1914, a group called the Santa Claus Association was formed in New York City to perpetuate the Santa myth. One thing the group did was respond to letters to Santa.

The jewelry store Birks had a very different type of store Santa in 1920. Birks made a jewel-encrusted Santa to attract customers. His suit was made of rubies with diamonds for the trim. The tuque was also made of rubies with a pearl and emerald trim. The lining was of sapphires. It cost $30,000 to make and stood eight inches tall. In the Dirty Thirties, it was disassembled to make bracelets.

In 1937, a professional Santa set up a training school in Albion, New York, called the Charles Howard Santa Claus School. Students enrolled in a week-long course that taught them, among other things, stories about Santa Claus, how toys are made and what parents and children expect from Santa Claus.

Other Santa Songs

Not all the songs that have been written about this jolly old fellow are as memorable as the above-mentioned. Indeed, some of them would be best forgotten.

 In 1946, Champion Jack Dupree recorded "Santa Claus Blues."

In 1959, Gene Autry recorded the forgettable "Santa's Comin' in a Whirlybird."

In 1963, Clyde Lasley and the Cadillac Baby Specials recorded "Santa Claus Came Home Drunk."

In 1966, Lorne Green recorded "Must Be Santa."

In 1971, the pot-loving pair of Cheech and Chong released their contribution to the mix—"Santa Claus and His Old Lady."

DID YOU KNOW?

The term "Santa Claus" comes from Saint Nicholas. Santa is a form of saint, and Claus is a shortened form of Nicholas.

Rudolph, the Red-Nosed Reindeer

Rudolph, the Red-Nosed Reindeer, that well-loved Christmas icon, grew out of the mind of Robert "Bob" May as a marketing gimmick for the Chicago department store Montgomery Ward in 1939. May chose to write about an outcast reindeer because as a youngster he had been teased for being shy and small for his age. It was May's four-year-old daughter who chose Rudolph as the name of his famous reindeer over Rollo and Reginald.

In 1946, Sewell Avery, chair of Montgomery Ward, transferred the Rudolph copyright to Bob May to help him cover his wife Evelyn's medical bills (she died of cancer in 1938) and the college tuition for his six children.

Bob May donated the original manuscript of his story "Rudolph, the Red-Nosed Reindeer" to Dartmouth College's Baker Library.

Singing about Rudolph

In 1949, Johnny Marks, Bob May's brother-in-law, wrote the song we are all familiar with. He had to establish his own music publishing company, St. Nicholas Music, to publish his song about May's reindeer because no existing company could be persuaded to publish a song about an advertising gimmick.

The first person approached to sing "Rudolph, the Red-Nosed Reindeer" was Perry Como. He agreed to record the song only if a line was changed. May and Marks refused. Bing Crosby and Dinah Shore were the next people approached to record Marks' song. Both singers chose not to do so. May and Marks next approached Gene Autry. He recorded the song only because his wife liked it; Rudolph reminded her of the Ugly Duckling.

When the song "Rudolph, the Red-Nosed Reindeer" was released in 1949, it was a huge hit, selling two million copies in the first year.

In 1956, the Cadillacs produced a doo-wop version of "Rudolph, the Red-Nosed Reindeer."

The Christmas Jug Band recorded a parody of the song called "Rudolph, the Bald-Headed Reindeer" in 1987.

DID YOU KNOW?

Only female reindeer still have their antlers by midwinter, so Santa's reindeer must all be girls!

Run Rudolph Run
Another song about Rudolph was released by Chuck Berry in 1958. Though in this well-known Christmas song Chuck Berry croons, "Run, run Rudolph," the song was entitled "Run Rudolph Run."

"Run Rudolph Run" has been played in several films, including *Cast Away* (2000), *Diner* (1982), *Home Alone* (1990), *Deck the Halls* (2006), *Stealing Christmas* (2003), *Jingle All the Way* (1996), and *The Santa Clause 2* (2002).

DID YOU KNOW?

A red nose in a reindeer is the result of an infection by a parasite.

Reindeer Boogie
Canadian country music singer and yodeler Clarence Eugene "Hank" Snow (1914–1999) recorded "Reindeer Boogie" in the 1950s. Trisha Yearwood also released a version of "Reindeer Boogie."

DID YOU KNOW?

In 2001, the island of Jersey printed a Christmas stamp showing Santa and his reindeer with a group of carolers.

Leroy, the Redneck Reindeer
"Leroy, the Redneck Reindeer" was released in 1995 on country singer Joe Diffie's *Mr. Christmas* album. In the song, Leroy is asked to fill in for Rudolph, who is ill. However, rather than pull Santa's sleigh, Leroy drives a pickup truck full of toys. Leroy wears overalls and a John Deere tractor cap.

DID YOU KNOW?

In Louisiana, Rudolph, the Red-Nosed Reindeer and the rest of Santa's team of reindeer are replaced by a team of alligators led by a red-nosed werewolf.

Frosty the Snowman

"Frosty the Snowman" was written by Steve Nelson and Jack Rollins in 1950. It was an attempt to cash in on the success of another popular Christmas character, Rudolph, the Red-Nosed Reindeer. The song by that name had been released a year earlier and had sold very well.

"Frosty the Snowman" was first recorded by Gene Autry in 1951, when it became the best-selling Christmas record. As a result of the song's success, Frosty the Snowman quickly became a popular holiday figure. Sears, Roebuck and Company made Frosty a seasonal mascot of the company, stocking all types of Frosty merchandise. Dell Comics published yearly Frosty the Snowman comics.

The animated TV movie based on the song appeared in 1969. It was narrated by Jimmy Durante. Durante's recording of the song is the best-known version today. The movie led to the release of its own soundtrack album. In the sequel *Frosty Returns* (1992), Frosty and the little girl sing "Let There Be Snow."

🔔 The singing duo of Jan Berry and Dean Torrence recorded a doo-wop version of "Frosty the Snowman" in 1962.

🔔 The 1997 holiday CD *A Funky Little Christmas* included a reggae "Frosty the Sno Mon."

The Chipmunks

Ross Bagdasarian, an Armenian American songwriter, wrote and recorded "The Chipmunk Song (Christmas Don't Be Late)" in 1958. After recording the song, Ross Bagdasarian had his voice speeded up to give it that chipmunk-like sound. That same year, he changed his name to David Seville, the name of his character. The three fictitious chipmunk singers introduced in the song are named Alvin, Simon and Theodore. All three have gone on to have very successful careers beyond the Christmas season and are still popular characters today.

🔔 "The Chipmunk Song" sold over 4.5 million copies in the first seven weeks after its release in 1958. It is the only Christmas tune that has ever been number one in the United States on Christmas Day.

🔔 "The Chipmunk Song (Christmas Don't Be Late)" won three Grammy awards in 1958: best comedy performance, best children's recording and best engineered record (non-classical).

🔔 In 1962, the Chipmunks released their first Christmas LP, *Christmas with the Chipmunks*.

🔔 In 1963, the second Chipmunks Christmas LP came out, *Christmas with the Chipmunks, vol. 2*.

🔔 "The Chipmunk Song" has appeared in two movies: *Donnie Brasco* (1997) and *Almost Famous* (2000).

🔔 When the movie *Alvin and the Chipmunks* was released in 2007, "The Chipmunk Song" hit the Billboard's Top 100 chart once again.

DID YOU KNOW?

Ross Bagdasarian could neither read nor write music.

Dominick the Italian Christmas Donkey

In 1960, Ray Allen, Sam Saltzberg and Wandra Merrell collaborated on a unique Christmas song. It was about a donkey who comes to Santa's aid in Italy, where the rocky hills and mountains are too difficult for his reindeer to climb. His name was Dominick the Italian Christmas Donkey.

The song of the same name was first recorded by the Italian American novelty singer Lou Monte (born Lou Scaglione). Production of the recording was financed by the Gambino family, members of the New York Mafia. The song was re-released in 2011 and did very well in Britain. Dominick the Donkey has become a well-known symbol of Christmas in Italy.

Characters that Didn't Catch On
In 1952, Stuart Hamblin released "The Three Little Dwarfs." This was a song about Santa's helpers, named Hardrock, Coco and Joe. Somebody must have forgotten to tell Hamblin that Santa's helpers are elves, not dwarfs.

Jimmy Dean also attempted to introduce a new Christmas character from which to profit. In 1957, he released the forgettable song "Little Sandy Sleighfoot" about an elf with very big feet. He is unable to help Santa in his workshop, but when the reindeer stable burns down, he helps Santa to deliver toys with his ski feet.

MORE SONGS FOR CHILDREN

All I Want for Christmas Is My Two Front Teeth

"All I Want for Christmas Is My Two Front Teeth" was written by Don Gardner (1913–2004), a music teacher in Smithtown, New York, in 1946. Gardner got the idea for the song when he noticed that many of his grade two students lisped when they said "Merry Christmas" because they were missing at least one of their front teeth. It took him only half an hour to write the lyrics.

When Spike Jones and the City Slickers performed "All I Want for Christmas Is My Two Front Teeth" in 1948, it was the chubby trumpeter George Rock who did the singing dressed in short pants with his two front teeth blackened. After singing the song, George Rock received thousands of teeth, two at a time, in the mail from fans.

The most popular Christmas song of 1948 was "All I Want for Christmas Is My Two Front Teeth." It was a top 10 hit again in 1955, this time sung by seven-year-old Barry Gordon.

"All I Want for Christmas Is My Two Front Teeth" has been recorded by several other artists, including Mariah Carey, George Strait and Nat King Cole. Alvin and the Chipmunks did their own unique version.

There have also been several parodies of the song over the years. Homer and Jethro released a parody of this song in 1968—"All I Want for Christmas is My Upper Plate." Singer and drag performer RuPaul released a parody of this holiday song on the Christmas album *Ho, Ho, Ho* in 1997. In it, the singer wants plastic surgery, not two front teeth, for Christmas. On the 2002 holiday album *Cledus Navidad*, the song is parodied by singer Cledus T. Judd as "All I Want for Christmas Is Two Gold Front Teef."

DID YOU KNOW?

Spike Jones, whose band first recorded "All I Want for Christmas Is My Two Front Teeth," was really named Lindley. He got his nickname because as a teenager, he was very skinny. His father's coworkers at the railway would compare him to a railway spike.

Holiday Songs by Tepper and Bennett

The New York song-writing duo of Sid Tepper and Roy C. Bennett was very prolific, writing songs for many famous musicians including Frank Sinatra, Elvis Presley and The Beatles. During their long partnership, the men also wrote two Christmas songs—"Suzy Snowflake" and "I'm Gettin' Nuttin' for Christmas."

Suzy Snowflake

"Suzy Snowflake" was written in 1951 by Tepper and Bennett, who dedicated it to the Teppers' new baby daughter, Susan. The song is about a girl in a white gown—the snowflake—who happily plays in her snowy world with all who will join her.

"Suzy Snowflake" was first recorded in 1951 by Rosemary Clooney for Columbia Records.

DID YOU KNOW?

Only one percent of all snowflakes are symmetrical.

I'm Gettin' Nuttin' for Christmas

Tepper and Bennett wrote "I'm Gettin' Nuttin' for Christmas" in 1955. It was inspired by an incident involving Bennett's daughter Claire spilling ink on the carpet; her mother told her that she would not be getting anything for Christmas if her behavior did not improve. The pranks mentioned in the song were those pulled by the children of the two men.

This amusing piece was recorded by five separate artists in 1955, each version appearing on the pop charts—Barry Gordon's and Art Mooney's both at number 6; Joe Ward's at number 20; Ricky Zahnd and the Blue Jeaners' at number 21; and Stan Freberg's at number 55. Surprisingly, it is Freberg's rendition that is best known today.

I Want a Hippopotamus for Christmas

John Rox (1902–1957) wrote one of the quirkiest holiday songs ever: "I Want a Hippopotamus for Christmas." It was first recorded by 10-year-old Oklahoma native Gayla Peevey in 1953. An Oklahoma man harnessed the song's popularity and called upon people to send in their nickels and dimes to buy the young singer a real hippopotamus for Christmas. He succeeded in raising enough money and Gayla was presented with a baby hippo, which she in turn donated to the Oklahoma City Zoo.

Telus, a Canadian communications company, used this holiday song (and hippos) in commercials in 2005 and 2011.

Young Gayla Peevey recorded two other Christmas songs, neither of which caught on—"Angel in a Christmas Play" and "Got a Cold in My Nose for Christmas." A few years later, at the age of 16, Gayla Peevey changed her name to Jamie Horton.

I Saw Mommy Kissing Santa Claus

Songwriter Tommie Connor wrote "I Saw Mommy Kissing Santa Claus." It was first recorded in 1952 by 13-year-old Jimmy Boyd and became the most popular Christmas tune of that year, selling over two million copies.

It was "underneath the mistletoe" that the singer saw Mommy kissing Santa Claus. Kissing under the mistletoe is a popular English holiday custom with a long history. In Charles Dickens' tale *The Pickwick Papers* (1837), Mr. Pickwick finds himself under the mistletoe at a party on Christmas Eve. He is immediately grabbed and kissed by each of a group of young ladies. This is known to have been part of Christmas celebrations for hundreds of years before Dickens wrote about it. In areas of the country where mistletoe was not easy to find, a substitute was constructed by crossing two hoops adorned with greenery such as holly or ivy.

Each time you kiss someone under a sprig of mistletoe, you are supposed to remove one of the berries. When the berries are all gone, so are all the kisses. It was believed that a woman who did not get kissed under the mistletoe would not marry in the upcoming year.

Magical Mistletoe

Mistletoe grows as a parasite on trees rather than from the ground. Many groups of people have attributed magical powers to the plant because of this, including the early Celtic religious leaders known as Druids. (They, however, limited these powers to mistletoe that grew on oak trees.) But it may be through the Vikings that we get our tradition of kissing each other under the mistletoe at Christmastime.

According to Norse mythology, the goddess Frigga gave birth to a son named Balder, whom she protected from everything on the earth or under the earth. When Balder grew up, he became enemies with another god, Loki. Loki realized that mistletoe neither grew from the earth nor was found under the earth, but rather grew from a tree. He made a spear tipped with mistletoe and cast it at Balder, whose heart was pierced, killing him. Frigga's tears for her son turned into the plant's white berries. Eventually, Balder was restored to life. Overjoyed, Frigga began the custom of kissing anyone who stood under mistletoe.

DID YOU KNOW?

Central Texas produces 95 percent of the world's mistletoe.

More Mistletoe Music

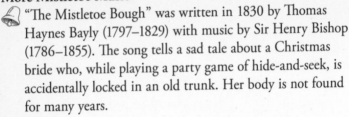

🔔 "The Mistletoe Bough" was written in 1830 by Thomas Haynes Bayly (1797–1829) with music by Sir Henry Bishop (1786–1855). The song tells a sad tale about a Christmas bride who, while playing a party game of hide-and-seek, is accidentally locked in an old trunk. Her body is not found for many years.

🔔 "Mistletoe and Holly" was recorded by Frank Sinatra in 1957. Sinatra wrote the song with Hank Sanicola and Doc Stanford. Faith Evans released a version in 2005.

🔔 Aretha Franklin released "Kissin' by the Mistletoe" in 1961.

🔔 In 1969, Isaac Hayes recorded "The Mistletoe and Me."

🔔 "Mistletoe and Wine" is a song written by Jeremy Paul, Leslie Stewart and Keith Strachan in 1976 for the musical *Scraps,* which was based on the Hans Christian Andersen story *The Little Matchgirl.* The song's lyrics are packed with all the traditional niceties of the season. It was sung when the well-to-do partygoers evicted the poor, starving little matchgirl from the building and into the wintry snow. When the musical was made into a television movie entitled *The Little Matchgirl* in 1986, the song was sung by Twiggy, the former British model. Cliff Richards rewrote the lyrics and put a more religious bent to them before releasing it as a single in 1988. "Mistletoe and Wine" has become very popular in Britain.

🔔 "It Must Have Been the Mistletoe" was Barbara Mandrell's new Christmas song for 1984. It was written by Justin Wilde and Doug Konecky. The song was on the soundtrack for the 2000 television movie *Once Upon a Christmas.*

🔔 In 1989, Randy Travis recorded the country song "Meet Me Under the Mistletoe," written by Mark Abramson, Betty Jackson and Joe Collins.

"Mistletoe" was written by Colbie Caillat and Stacy Blue in 2007 and recorded by Colbie Caillat. This song was featured in two films in 2008—*Baby Mama* and *Christmas Child*.

Another song entitled "Mistletoe" was on Canadian singer Justin Bieber's 2011 Christmas album *Under the Mistletoe*.

Disney Sings Christmas

Not surprisingly, Walt Disney was quick to join Christmas' consumer cash grab. Beginning with a one-hour holiday special in 1950, Disney embraced the season in a variety of musical ways. Popular Christmas songs were recorded by Disney's favorite characters. Some new songs were written as well. Many of these were well received by the youngsters of the day, but not all. Even Disney has produced some flops.

Sonny Burke and Peggy Lee wrote "Peace on Earth" for Disney's 1955 *Lady and the Tramp*. It occurs at both the beginning and the end of the movie, showing Christmas at Darling and Jim Dear's—first with only Lady and a year later with Tramp and the puppies, too.

In 1957, Disney released the record *Walt Disney's Christmas Concert* starring the fictional characters Ludwig Mousensky and the All-Mouse Orchestra. Pre-dating Alvin and the Chipmunks by a year, the record was a flop. Released with no real context, consumers did not understand the poorly done "mouse" sounds.

The wicked queen cackles "Jingle Bones," a new version of an old favorite, over the holiday season to participants on Fantasyland's Snow White ride.

"Oh, What a Merry Christmas Day" was written by Irwin Kostal (music) and Frederick Searles (lyrics) for Disney's 1983 *Mickey's Christmas Carol*. It lists some joys of the season.

 In Disney's *The Muppet Christmas Carol* (1992), Kermit the Frog as Bob Cratchit and some book-keeping rats sing Paul Williams' "One More Sleep Till Christmas" while closing up the shop after Scrooge leaves on Christmas Eve.

DID YOU KNOW?

Two of Guyana's Disney-themed Christmas stamps featured characters caroling. On one stamp, the singers were Mickey and Minnie Mouse, Donald Duck, Pluto and Goofy. On the other stamp, Mickey Mouse sings with some mice.

MISCELLANEOUS MUSIC

The Holiday Blues

Not everyone looks forward to the holiday season. People who are separated from family and friends and will be spending the day alone often dread the approach of a day that does little but accent their loneliness. Still other people who have little money can become depressed by all the emphasis on extravagant gift-giving that cries out from a multitude of advertising media. Many people find that December can become extremely stressful with all the preparations to be made for the holidays and the crowds to contend with everywhere. There is a group of Christmas songs that acknowledges these less than merry feelings that Christmas can elicit. Elvis Presley's recording of "Blue Christmas" is the best-known.

Blue Christmas

 "Blue Christmas" was written by a frustrated and depressed middle-aged man named Jay Johnson on a dismal early winter's day in 1939. Billy Hayes wrote the music for the song.

Ernest Tubb, the Texas Troubadour, recorded "Blue Christmas" in 1949. It reached number one. In 1950 and 1951, it was number two.

Elvis Presley recorded "Blue Christmas" in 1957. This carol proved to be a hit for the singing sensation, but it was never his favorite. Presley preferred his recording of "If Every Day Was Like Christmas."

More Sad Songs
Two African American blues Christmas songs are "I Want a Present for Christmas" and "Good Morning Blues (I Want to See Santa Claus)."

Here are a number of other sad Christmas songs. How many of them have you heard?

"(It's Gonna Be A) Lonely Christmas" (The Orioles, 1948)

"Empty Stocking Blues" (Floyd Dixon, 1951)

"Just a Lonely Christmas" (The Moonglows, 1953)

"My Christmas Blues" (Lil Esther and Mel Walker, 1954)

"Christmas Hard Times" (Redd Foxx, 1959)

"Blues for Christmas" (John Lee Hooker, 1960)

"Christmas (Baby Please Come Home)" (Darlene Love, 1963)

"Christmas Will Be Just Another Day" (Brenda Lee, 1964)

"Such a Lonely Time of Year" (Nancy Sinatra, 1969)

"Christmas Eve Can Kill You" (The Everly Brothers, 1972)

"Who Took the Merry Out of Christmas?" (The Staple Singers, 1973)

"What Do the Lonely Do at Christmas?" (The Emotions, 1973)

 "Christmas Shoes" (Newsong, 2000)

It's a Rhythm-and-Blues Christmas!

"Merry Christmas, Baby" and "Please Come Home for Christmas" made Charles Brown the best-known blues and rhythm-and-blues Christmas singer.

Merry Christmas, Baby

"Merry Christmas, Baby" is a blues song written by Lou Baxter and Johnny Moore. Johnny Moore's Three Blazers were the first to record it in 1947. Elvis Presley, Chuck Berry and B.B. King have also recorded this song.

"Merry Christmas, Baby" has been featured twice on the *A Very Special Christmas* series—Bruce Springsteen and the E Street Band sang it for the original album in 1987, and Bonnie Raitt and Charles Brown did a duet for the second album in 1992.

Charles Brown performs "Merry Christmas, Baby" on the soundtrack for the 1996 movie *Jingle All the Way*. The band Hanson performed it for the 1998 movie *Jack Frost*. "Merry Christmas, Baby" is also included on the soundtrack for the 2002 movie *Friday After Next*.

"Merry Christmas, Baby" was included on the 2006 album *The Muppets: A Green and Red Christmas*. The muppet Pepe the King Prawn was the singer.

Please Come Home for Christmas

"Please Come Home for Christmas" was written by Charles Brown (who was the first to record it in 1960) and Gene Redd. It was number one on the Christmas charts in 1972.

The Eagles recorded "Please Come Home for Christmas" in 1978.

"Please Come Home for Christmas" (performed by Southside Johnny Lyon) was a very appropriate song to be included in the 1990 movie *Home Alone* about a young boy (played by Macaulay Caulkin) who accidentally gets left behind at home when his family leaves for Christmas vacation.

In 1991, Pat Benatar recorded "Please Come Home for Christmas" and released it to the American troops serving in the Gulf War.

Jon Bon Jovi released a version of the song in 1992. Model Cindy Crawford starred in the accompanying video.

Jonell Mosser recorded the song for the 1993 movie *Look Who's Talking Now*. In 2003, Sawyer Brown's version of "Please Come Home for Christmas" was used in the movie *Bad Santa*.

Caroling with a Latin Beat

Mary's Boy Child

In 1956, the African American composer Jester Hairston wrote the calypso-style song "Mary's Boy Child" for his friend Harry Belafonte. In 1957, Harry Belafonte had a number one Christmas hit with the song.

In 1978, Boney M also scored a number one Christmas hit with a remake of this song entitled "Mary's Boy Child—Oh My Lord."

St. Kitts issued a miniature sheet of Christmas stamps in 1983 featuring the song "Mary's Boy Child."

Feliz Navidad

 "Feliz Navidad" is a Christmas song written and recorded by Puerto Rican singer José Feliciano in 1970. It has lyrics in both Spanish and English.

The Arrows did a version of "Feliz Navidad" for the 2004 movie *Christmas with the Kranks*.

Feliz Navidad means "Merry Christmas" in Spanish.

Q: What do Mexican sheep sing at Christmas?

A: Fleece Navidad!

Calypso Carol

"Calypso Carol" was written by an English seminary student named Michael Perry (1942–1996) in 1964. Perry was one of the most successful hymn writers of the past century.

"Calypso Carol" became widely known through a chance occurrence: it was chosen to replace a missing piece of music for singing sensation Cliff Richards' radio programme.

"Calypso Carol" was featured on a miniature sheet of Christmas stamps by Nevis in 1983.

Mama Bake the Johnny Cake

"Mamma Bake the Johnny Cake" is traditional Christmas song in St. Croix, U.S. Virgin Islands.

A Johnny cake is not actually a cake at all. It is a flatbread made from cornmeal.

Pretty Paper

Singer Willie Nelson wrote songs for both himself and other artists to perform. "Pretty Paper," written by Nelson, was originally recorded by Roy Orbison in 1963. Nelson himself recorded "Pretty Paper" in 1978. More recently, Randy Travis, Kenny Chesney, Chris Isaak and Carly Simon have all recorded "Pretty Paper."

The song is about how people get caught up in themselves and their own lives and fail to notice those around them. It speaks to how buying gifts and pretty wrapping paper has become more important for many people during the holiday season (and thence the rest of the year also) than helping their less fortunate fellows.

The Gift of Music

The exchange of gifts around the time of the Winter Solstice has a very long history, pre-dating Christianity by thousands of years.

The Babylonians, at their New Year's festival of Zagmuk, gave gifts to each other, as did the Romans at their solstice celebration, the Saturnalia. For Christians, the practice of secret gift giving began in the 12th century when French nuns, inspired by stories of Saint Nicholas, left presents at the homes of poor children on December 5, the eve of St. Nicholas Day (December 6). Today, young and old alike give and receive gifts on Christmas Day.

At least three children over the years have received unique and special gifts—Christmas songs written especially for them.

🔔 "Christians, Awake, Salute the Happy Morn" was written by John Byrom (1692–1763) in 1749 as a Christmas gift for his daughter Dorothy (Dolly). At the top of the original manuscript is written, "Christmas Day for Dolly."

🔔 Between 1874 and 1876, the musician Franz Liszt (1811–1886) wrote and combined 12 movements into a composition called "Christmas Tree Suite" (*Weihnachtsbaum*). It was first published in 1882, when it was dedicated to his granddaughter Daniela von Bülow.

🔔 Roger Miller (1936–1992) wrote the song "Old Toy Trains" (1967) as a Christmas gift for his son Dean. As an adult, Dean Miller (who is also a songwriter) would remember it as the best Christmas present he ever received.

DID YOU  KNOW?

The first toy trains were made in the mid-19th century out of wood or metal.

Prayers for Peace

Do You Hear What I Hear?

"Do You Hear What I Hear?" was a prayer for peace written during the Cuban Missile Crisis in October 1962 and was recorded by the Harry Simeone Chorale that same year.

Noël Regney, a Frenchman living in the U.S., suffered from bouts of depression as a result of his experiences during World War II. American involvement in Korea and then Vietnam made his depression worse, and to combat it, Regney wrote a Christmas poem that focused on his deep desire for peace on earth. It was called "Do You Hear What I Hear?" His wife, Gloria Shayne, composed the music. "Do You Hear What I Hear?" was created in the opposite manner of how the couple usually wrote songs; Gloria normally wrote the lyrics and Noël the music.

The song has proven to be popular with both listeners and singers alike. A large number of artists have recorded the hit, including Bing Crosby, Perry Como, Pat Boone, Glen Campbell, Martina McBride, Anne Murray and Whitney Houston.

Happy Xmas (War is Over)

"Happy Xmas (War is Over)" was written in 1971 by former Beatles member John Lennon and his wife, Yoko Ono. They recorded it with the Harlem Community Choir. It was a song protesting American involvement in the Vietnam War.

The background lyrics, "War is over, if you want it, war is over, now!" had appeared a year earlier on billboard ads in major American cities. The ads were paid for by John and Yoko.

Talk about Not Deserving Any Presents…

In December 1964, a group of Congolese rebels massacred some white missionaries and priests. After the blood-letting, the rebels serenaded the survivors with Christmas carols.

DID YOU KNOW?

"Snoopy's Christmas" (1967) by the Royal Guardsmen uses the story of the Christmas Truce of 1914.

Christmas Music for the Movies

Have Yourself a Merry Little Christmas

The movie *Meet Me in St. Louis* (1944) tells of a family's move from Missouri to New York City. In it, Esther, the big sister, sings a song to her younger sister, Tootie, who is worried that Santa will not be able to find her in their new home. Hugh Martin and Ralph Blane, the songwriters for the movie, had written a song with sad lyrics for the star Judy Garland to sing: "Have yourself a merry little Christmas; it may be your last; next year we will be living in the past." Garland refused to sing the song as it was, stating it was too depressing for war time, so a new, more optimistic version was written: "Have yourself a merry little Christmas; let your heart be light; from now on our troubles will be out of sight."

"Have Yourself a Merry Little Christmas" has expressed its holiday wishes in several other movies, such as *Home Alone* (1990), *Surviving Christmas* (2004), *The Godfather* (1972), *The Holiday* (2006), *Obsessed* (2009), *While You Were Sleeping* (1995), *Bad Santa* (2003), *Dirty Dancing: Havana Nights* (2004), *Donnie Brasco* (1997), *High Crimes* (2002) and *When Harry Met Sally* (1989).

You're a Mean One, Mr. Grinch

Dr. Seuss (Theodore Seuss Geisel) (1904–1991), the beloved children's author, wrote the story *How the Grinch Stole Christmas* in 1957. The 1966 animated cartoon based upon Dr. Seuss' *How the Grinch Stole Christmas* launched the holiday tune, "You're a Mean One, Mr. Grinch," sung by Thurl Ravenscroft (who is also the voice of Kellogg's Frosted Flakes' Tony the Tiger). The song was co-written by Dr. Seuss and Albert Hague. Other than the one song, the voice of the Grinch was done by Boris Karloff. A full-length movie version of the story was released in 2000 with Jim Carrey starring as the Grinch.

Some More Holiday Songs Introduced in the Movies

"Holly Jolly Christmas" was written by Johnny Marks and sung by Burl Ives in the 1964 animated special *Rudolph, the Red-Nosed Reindeer*.

The well-known ditty "We Need a Little Christmas" was written by Jeremy Herman for the Broadway musical *Mame* (1966). The musical was made into a movie in 1974. Mame, the title character, sings the song to cheer people up after the stock market crash.

In the 2000 movie version of the classic *How the Grinch Stole Christmas*, little Cindy Lou Who (Taylor Momsen) sings "Christmas, Why Can't I Find You?" It was written for the movie by James Horner and Will Jennings. A longer version of the song, "Where Are You, Christmas?" was written by Horner and Jennings along with Mariah Carey. Carey was unable to release the song because of legal disputes with her ex-husband Tommy Mottola, so country singer Faith Hill recorded it instead.

Hilary Duff's single "Santa Claus Lane" debuted in *The Santa Clause 2* in 2002. Aly & AJ's "Greatest Time of the Year" was first featured in the sequel, *The Santa Clause 3: The Escape Clause*, in 2006.

"Christmas Is All Around" is a parody of the song "Love Is All Around." It is sung by the character Billy Mack (played by Bill Nighy) in an attempt to regain some of his former fame in the 2003 movie *Love Actually*.

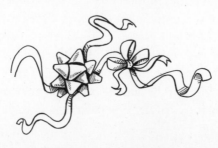

Carols about Christmas Cake

Christmas fruit cake—love it or hate it, it seems there simply is no middle ground. This black-and-white attitude about this holiday dessert is captured in two seasonal songs; the Victorian "Miss Hooligan's Christmas Cake" (1883) and the contemporary "The Same Christmas Cake" (1998).

In the earlier song by C. Frank Horn, Miss Hooligan has baked a cake of which she is very proud for the holidays. She is invites her neighbors over to have a piece of the cake. Unable to get out of eating a piece of the rock-hard delight, the company all ends up sick. "Miss Hooligan's Christmas Cake" became popular in Newfoundland and Labrador in the 1940s when recorded by the McNulty Family in 1941 under the slightly different title of "Miss Fogarty's Christmas Cake."

In the Canadian band The Arrogant Worms' modern tune, the cake is an old one passed down through the family and is seemingly as indestructible as Miss Hooligan's cake.

Apparently, a fruit cake that contains alcohol, such as rum or whisky, will remain edible for many years. (Scottish Christmas cakes are often made with whisky while the people of Canada's Prince Edward Island generally sprinkle their fruitcakes with rum and brandy.) A family in Tecumseh, Michigan, owns a cake that has been in the family since 1878. Jay Leno of *The Tonight Show* sampled it on television in 2003.

Special desserts have long been served at Christmas whenever possible, but until the 16th century, the only people in the northern parts of Europe able to eat fruit during the winter months were the very wealthy. With the creation of sugar cane plantations in the Caribbean and the realization that fruit could be preserved with sugar, it became possible for more people to enjoy fruit (and sugar) during the cold winter months. Thus, the Christmas fruitcake became a popular holiday tradition.

DID YOU KNOW?

In the U.S., December 27 is National Fruitcake Day and December is National Fruitcake Month.

Sexually Suggestive Season's Greetings

As with any festive occasion, sex (whether through innuendo or action) is frequently part of the mix. Sexually suggestive Christmas songs are nothing new. One thing that has changed over time, though, is the explicitness of the lyrics—the sexual nature of the song once conveyed through double entendres and tone of voice is now often point-blank.

🔔 "Christmas Balls" (1936) recorded by Ben Light and the Surf Club Boys is full of double entendres and was one of the first in a long line of humorous Christmas jingles.

🔔 In 1949, Amos Milburn encouraged his lady, "Let's Make Christmas Merry Baby."

🔔 In 1950, jazz singer Ella Fitzgerald released the risqué "Santa Claus Got Stuck in My Chimney." This song may have been dreamt up in response to the lyrics in Milburn's song of a year earlier, in which he sings about wanting to "slide down your chimney and fill your stocking full of toys." As her popularity as a singer spread, Fitzgerald and her lawyers successfully got the song's distribution blocked. It was not re-released until 1996.

🔔 "Santa Baby" was co-written by Joan Javits, Phil Springer and Tony Springer. The lyrics suggest pillow-talk between a woman and her sugar daddy. Eartha Kitt took "Santa Baby" to number one in 1953. Many female singers have recorded the sultry song over the years, including Madonna,

Kylie Minogue, LeAnn Rimes, Taylor Swift, Brittney Spears and Shakira.

🔔 In 1954, Jimmy Butler sang about sprinkling his snow on his woman's evergreen in "Trim Your Tree."

🔔 The ribald "Back Door Santa" was first recorded by Clarence Carter in 1968. Bon Jovi did a version in 1987. In this sexually suggestive song, Santa "keeps all the little girls happy while the boys are out to play."

🔔 AC/DC's contribution to the list of naughty Christmas songs is "I Want a Mistress for Christmas." It appeared on the group's 1990 album *The Razor's Edge*.

🔔 In 2008, Lady Gaga released "Christmas Tree," sung to the tune of "Deck the Halls." Its sexually suggestive lyrics were met with mixed reviews.

I Want You for Christmas

There have been many, many Christmas songs written over the centuries. Some have struck a chord in the hearts of listeners and have survived the test of time. Others are just better forgotten. This next group of carols is just that. Most were written at the beginning of the rock-and-roll era (1964 was clearly the height of Beatlemania), though at least one is from the 1990s. Each one identifies a celebrity as the object of the singer's affection and as the top item on the singer's Christmas wish list:

🔔 "I Want Eddie Fisher for Christmas" (Spike Jones, 1954)

🔔 "I Want Elvis for Christmas" (Holly Twins, 1956)

🔔 "Elvis for Christmas" (Mad Milo, 1957)

🔔 "All I Want for Christmas is a Beatle" (Dora Bryan, 1963)

🔔 "Bring Me a Beatle for Christmas" (Cindy Rella, 1964)

🔔 "Christmas with The Beatles" (Judy & the Duets, 1964)

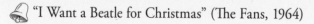

🔔 "I Want a Beatle for Christmas" (The Fans, 1964)

🔔 "I Want a Beatle for Christmas" (Becky Lee Beck, 1964)

🔔 "(I Want a) Beatle for Christmas" (Patty Surbey & the Canadian VIPs, 1964)

🔔 "Ringo Bells" (Three Blonde Mice, 1964)

🔔 "Santa Bring Me Ringo" (Christine Hunter, 1964)

🔔 "Dear Santa (Bring Me a Man This Christmas)" (The Weather Girls, 1983)

🔔 "All I Want for Christmas is a Spice Girl" (Paul Griggs, 1997)

If you could put someone on the top of your Christmas wish list, who would it be?

Parodying Christmas

Many alternate versions or parodies of Christmas songs have been sung over the years. Indeed, the tradition is probably almost as old as the songs themselves. Just think back to schoolyard jingles like "Jingle bells, Batman smells, Robin laid an egg…." Some people, however, have been especially prolific at producing parodies of Christmas songs.

Metro

Metro is a Western Canadian comedian who has been performing since the 1960s. In the 1970s, he starred on the television show *The Cottonpickers*. Currently, he is the star of *The Metro Show*. Metro is a Ukrainian immigrant farmer whose material is life on the Prairies. He has produced numerous albums, including two Christmas ones: *The Eleven Days from Christmas* (1975) and *Metro's Next to Last Christmas Album* (2008). The first album made Canadian gold record standing and includes such songs as "Walkin' in My Winter Underwear" and "Chesnik Roasting on an Open Fire" (*chesnik* meaning "garlic"). The second album has many humorous musical parodies, including "Rockin' Around the Curling Rink" and "Have a Holly, Jolly Harvest."

Bob Rivers
Bob Rivers is a radio personality in Seattle. He is well known throughout the Pacific Northwest. He has been making Christmas parody albums since 1987. His first album, *Twisted Christmas*, made it to gold status. It included songs such as "The Twelve Pains of Christmas," which recounts the less joyful aspects of preparing for the holidays, and "Wreck the Malls." Next came *I am Santa Claus* in 1993 with "Walkin' Around in Women's Underwear" and "Teddy, the Red-Nosed Senator" (about Senator Teddy Kennedy, an alcoholic). In 1997 he released *More Twisted Christmas*, featuring "It's the Most Fattening Time of the Year" and "Yellow Snow! Yellow Snow! Yellow Snow!" The new millenium saw the release of *Chipmunks Roasting on an Open Fire* (2000), and *White Trash Christmas* (2002) with "Shoppin' Around for a Christmas Tree."

DID YOU KNOW?

Michael Powers released three blues twists of popular Christmas songs—"Mississippi Strummer Boy," "God Rest Ye Funky Gentlemen" and "Frosty the Bluesman."

More Miscellaneous Music

What Christmas Means to Me

"What Christmas Means to Me" was written in 1967 by Anna Gordy Gaye, George Gordy and Allen Story. Stevie Wonder had a hit in 1976 with the song. It was his version that was used in the 2002 movie *Reindeer Games* and in the 2003 movie *Elf.*

🔔 The song has been recorded by several artists, including Paul Young (1992) and Jessica Simpson (2004). It was used in a 2005 episode of the television series *Everybody Hates Chris.*

Merry Christmas Everybody

In 1973, the British rock band Slade released the holiday single "Merry Christmas Everybody." It sold 300,000 copies on the very first day and became Slade's best-selling single ever, reaching number one on the UK holiday charts that year.

The song was written by Slade vocalist Noddy Holder and bass guitarist Jimmy Lea. A song called "My Rocking Chair," also written by Holder, served as the basis for "Merry Christmas Everybody."

🔔 The year 1973 was a tough year economically in Britain, with many strikes occurring. The song was meant to cheer people up and have them look forward to a better future.

🔔 Slade recorded "Merry Christmas Everybody" at the Record Plant Studios in New York City. The chorus was recorded in the stairwell of the building to achieve the desired echo. The howl in the song was taken from a recording of Noddy Holder doing vocal exercises.

🔔 Slade drummer Don Powell was badly injured in a serious car accident a few months before the song was scheduled to be recorded. (His girlfriend, Angela Morris, was killed in the accident.) It left Powell with short-term memory loss. As a result, the song had to be recorded in bits.

"Merry Christmas Everybody" has been played on four episodes of the British television series *Dr. Who*: "The Christmas Invasion" (2005), "The Runaway Bride" (2006), "Turn Left" (2009) and "The End of Time" (2009).

Grandma Got Run Over by a Reindeer

Probably the most unlikely Christmas hit ever was "Grandma Got Run Over by a Reindeer." Written in 1978 by Randy Brooks and recorded a year later by the husband-and-wife singing duo of Elmo Shropshire and Patsy Trigg, the song has become the most requested Christmas song on the radio.

The song tells the tale of poor Grandma who drinks too much eggnog at the Christmas Eve festivities and then sets off walking home. Her body is later found, having been run over by Santa's reindeer. Grandpa does not seem overly upset and spends the next day celebrating Christmas as though nothing has happened. He does, however, now have a firm belief in the existence of Santa Claus.

Not surprisingly, this song was not well received in all circles. In Canada, numerous complaints to politicians were made by women's and seniors' groups, but to no avail. Indeed, the song was made into an animated children's movie in 2000 with a few child-friendly changes—Grandma does not die and Santa was not the person who hit her.

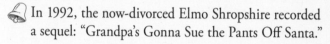 In 1992, the now-divorced Elmo Shropshire recorded a sequel: "Grandpa's Gonna Sue the Pants Off Santa."

Over the years, several parodies of this song have been written and recorded. In 1993, the band Da Yoopers recorded a parody of the song called "Grandpa Got Run Over by a Beer Truck." Another version has Grandpa being run over by a John Deere tractor. Bob Rivers made a parody of the song entitled "Osama Got Run Over by a Reindeer."

DID YOU KNOW?

Elmo and Patsy recorded another humorous Christmas song called "Percy, the Puny Poinsettia."

Wonderful Christmastime
Paul McCartney wrote and recorded this Christmas song in 1979. While a hit in Britain, it was not originally well received in the United States. McCartney has since expressed his displeasure with this song, which he terms "an embarassment."

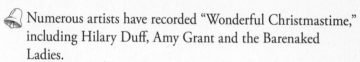 Numerous artists have recorded "Wonderful Christmastime," including Hilary Duff, Amy Grant and the Barenaked Ladies.

Peter Serafinowicz did a parody of the song on his television show, *The Peter Serafinowicz Show*: "Sexual Christmastime."

Last Christmas

"Last Christmas" was written by George Michael. The song was first recorded and released by Wham! in 1984.

🔔 The royalties from the first year of sales for "Last Christmas" were donated to Band Aid, the Ethiopian relief charity, as an out-of-court settlement resulting from the song's similarities to Barry Manilow's "Can't Smile without You."

🔔 Dalida recorded a French version of the song in 1984. A Polish version was released in 2005 by Andrzej Piaseczny, Mietek Szcześniak, Kuba Badach and Andrzej Lampert.

🔔 "Last Christmas" is very popular in Britain, Ireland, Finland, Norway, Austria, Germany and Australia.

🔔 This song was performed by the cast of the television show *Glee* on the episode "A Very Glee Christmas" in 2010.

Fairytale of New York

"Fairytale of New York," a popular song in Ireland and Britain, is not a typical Christmas song. It is neither light-hearted nor optimistic nor reverent. Indeed, in many ways, it is the exact opposite. And yet, it has been a success since it was first released in 1987 by the Celtic punk band The Pogues, with Kirsty MacColl, possibly because it helps people to put their own problems into perspective. The song's title was borrowed from the novel of the same name by James Patrick Donleavy, which inspired Shane MacGowan to write the song.

The song begins with a down-on-his-luck Irish immigrant to New York spending Christmas Eve in jail sleeping off a drinking binge. Another inmate begins singing an old Irish folk song, "The Rare Old Mountain Dew." The words make their way into the befuddled mind of the drunk and he begins to dream about his life in Ireland. The song is a duet between him and the female character in the folk song. It is a song about crushed dreams that ends in a loving reconciliation.

The song has been re-released by the band several times. The proceeds from the 2005 release were donated to several homeless charities. Proceeds were also given to Justice for Kirsty, a group devoted to discovering the truth behind a suspicious boating accident in Mexico in 2000 that claimed the life of Kirsty MacColl, the female vocalist who recorded "Fairytale of New York" with Shane MacGowan in 1987. Kirsty's mother Jean ended her campaign for justice in 2009 after the Mexican government closed the case.

"Fairytale of New York" was played in the opening scene of the 1996 movie *Basquiat* about the life of New York City artist Jean-Michel Basquiat. It was also played in the popular 2007 movie *P.S. I Love You*. It was heard on an episode of the television show *Being Erica*, as well.

The song has been recorded by numerous other artistis, including Sinéad O'Connor and Coldplay. Swedish and German versions of the song have also been released.

DID YOU KNOW?

The band name The Pogues is the Anglicized version of the Irish *póg mo thóin*, meaning "kiss my arse."

Other Christmas Albums
The original Christmas long-play album was Jimmy Wakely's 1949 *Christmas on the Range*. It was a country music record produced by Capitol Records.

One of the rarest (and hence most valuable) Christmas albums ever is The Moonglows' 1953 *Just a Lonely Christmas / Hey Santa Claus*.

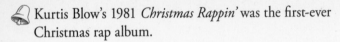

🔔 Kurtis Blow's 1981 *Christmas Rappin'* was the first-ever Christmas rap album.

🔔 Mariah Carey's 1994 album *Merry Christmas* is the best-selling Christmas album in history.

Q: What type of music do elves like best?

A: Wrap music!

PERFORMANCE PIECES

Bach's Christmas Oratorio

Johann Sebastian Bach (1685–1750) was born into a family of German musicians. As an adult, Bach was the cantor at Leipzig's St. Thomas Church. He wrote his *Christmas Oratorio BWV 248* for the parishioners there in 1734. It is actually a set of six cantatas, each pertaining to a different aspect of the Nativity story: "Introduction," "The Manger," "The Appearance of the Angel," "The Adoration before the Manger," "The Mystical Adoration" and "Final Hymns." Each section is approximately half an hour in length.

Bach's *Christmas Oratorio* was meant to be played one piece at a time on six different days: Christmas Day and the two following days, New Year's Day and the two following Sundays. It was first performed in six separate sections on various days between Christmas Day, 1734, and January 6, 1735, at two Leipzig churches—St. Thomas and St. Nicholas. It was not performed a second time until 1857 in Berlin.

Today, Bach's *Christmas Oratorio* is usually performed all at once rather than over six days. The Christmas lyrics of Paul Gerhardt, a 17th-century Berlin pastor, are often sung to the piece. Usually the chorus sings the part of the angels in Part II, the shepherds in Part III and the Wise Men in Part IV.

DID YOU KNOW?

Johann Sebastian Bach was the father of 20 children—seven with his first wife, Maria Barbara Bach, and 13 with his second wife, Anna Magdalena Wilcke. Only 10 lived to adulthood.

More Christmas Canatas

A cantata is a piece of music based upon a written text of some sort. It includes solo sections, duets, choruses and recitations. A number of cantatas, like Bach's grouping of six cantatas in his *Christmas Oratorio*, have been based upon a Christmas theme, usually the Nativity itself.

Czech Christmas Mass

In 1796, Jan Ryba (1765–1815), a well-known Czech composer, wrote a Christmas cantata called Česká mše vánoční ("Czech Christmas Mass"), designed to follow the structure of the Catholic mass. It is based upon the story of Jesus' birth but places it within a rural Czech setting. Ryba wrote both the lyrics and the music himself. This cantata is quite popular in the Czech Republic today at Christmastime. Indeed, it remains Ryba's most popular work.

The Star of Bethlehem

Josef Rheinberger (1839–1901) was a child musical prodigy whose father, treasurer of the Prince of Liechtenstein, initially opposed his son's desire for a musical career. He eventually relented, however, and his son went on to have a successful career as an organist, music teacher and composer. He wrote *Der Stern von Bethlehem* ("The Star of Bethlehem"), a Christmas cantata. It was based on a text written by his wife and former student, Franziska von Hoffnaass. Rheinberger's cantata was comprised of nine pieces: "Expectation," "The Shepherds," "The Appearance of the Angel," "Bethlehem," "The Shepherds at the Manger," "The Star," "Adoration of the Wise Men," "Mary" and "Fulfillment."

The Nativity

The Nativity is a cantata by American composer John Knowles Paine (1839–1906) based on text by John Milton (1608–1674). It is divided into three parts: "It Was the Winter Wild," "The Shepherds on the Lawn" and "Ring Out, Ye Crystal Spheres."

Fantasia on Christmas Carols

Ralph Vaughan Williams (1872–1958) was an English composer and collector of folk music. He was responsible for recording and publishing the lyrics of folk songs such as "The Sussex Carol" (see p. 60). In 1912, Williams decided to incorporate some of these folk carols into a Christmas cantata he called *Fantasia on Christmas Carols*. The folk carols he chose to include were "The Truth Sent from Above," "Come All You Worthy Gentlemen" and "On Christmas Night All Christians Sing." These were connected by snippets of "The First Nowell." The cantata was first performed at Hereford Cathedral at the Three Choirs Festival in 1912.

Christmas Story

Hugo Distler (1908–1942) was a talented musician and composer who had the misfortune of being an adult in Hitler's Nazi Germany. He was forced to join the Nazi Party in 1933 in order to retain his job in the music department of the Lübeck Conservatory. That same year, he wrote a cantata entitled *Weihnachtsgeschichte* ("Christmas Story"). It is based on "Lo, How a Rose E'er Blooming," a medieval German Christmas song that relates the Nativity events as told in Luke rather than the more common Matthew version. It was originally set to music by Michael Praetorius (1571–1621), who based his melody on an old German folk melody.

Distler, unfortunately, was to have a short life. He committed suicide in 1942 rather than be conscripted to fight in the Nazi army.

Saint Nicholas

Benjamin Britten (1913–1976) is best known for his Christmas piece called "A Ceremony of Carols" (see p. 169). However, he did compose another Christmas piece, a cantata entitled *Saint Nicholas*, in 1948. The text was written by Eric Crozier. It tells the life of St. Nicholas—"The Birth of St. Nicholas," "Nicholas Devotes Himself to God," "He Journeys to Palestine," "Nicholas Comes to Myra and is Chosen Bishop," "Nicholas from Prison," "Nicholas and the Pickled Boys," "His Piety and Marvellous Works" and "The Death of Nicholas."

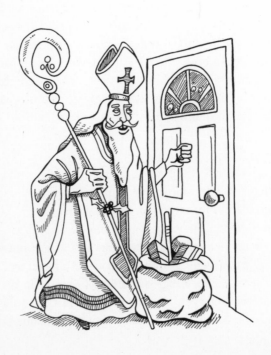

The Animals' Christmas

The Animals' Christmas is unique among cantatas in that it is not written in the classical style. Rather it is a pop piece written in 1986 by Jimmy Webb and Art Garfunkel. Garfunkel was a lead vocalist, along with Amy Grant, a Christian pop singer. The piece is divided into 12 sections: "The Annunciation," "The Creatures of the Field," "Just a Simple Little Tune," "The Decree," "Incredible Phat," "The Friendly Beasts," "The Song of the Camels," "Word from an Old Spanish Carol," "Carol of the Birds," "The Frog," "Herod" and "Wild Geese."

DID YOU KNOW?

There are six different Christmas songs called "Carol of the Birds." There is a medieval Catalonia tune, two 16th-century French songs, a Czech folk song, a song written in 1943 by John Jacob Niles, and an Australian song by John Wheeler and William Garnet Jones.

The Messiah

The Messiah was composed by George Frideric Handel (1685–1759) in 1741. It is divided into three parts pertaining to Jesus' birth, death and resurrection and is a type of musical composition known as an oratorio. This is a piece played by a full orchestra with vocal parts for several people. It is often built around a sacred story. *The Messiah* was originally performed at Easter.

Handel was inspired to write *The Messiah* by a collection of Biblical quotations sent to him by his friend Charles Jennens. When writing *The Messiah*, Handel locked himself in his room and did little else for two weeks. He slept and ate little, and when he did eat, he continued to compose at the same time. The smeared ink on several pages of his *Messiah* manuscript reveals the speed with which he wrote the piece.

The Messiah was first performed in Dublin in the spring of 1742. It was a fundraiser to benefit the Mercer's Hospital, prisoners in several jails and a local infirmary. Jonathon Swift, author of *Gulliver's Travels* and dean of Dublin's St. Patrick's Cathedral, originally refused to allow the members of his choir to participate in the production because it was to be given in a secular setting. Eventually, he relented. Also in that performance was Susanna Cibber of Dublin, who sang the contralto solo. She had been embroiled in a scandal, but her performance led the chancellor of St. Patrick's Cathedral to stand and shout, "Woman, for this all thy sins be forgiven."

The tradition of standing during *The Messiah*'s "Hallelujah Chorus" began in 1743 when King George II did so at the first London performance. No one knows why he stood up, but when the king stood, so too did everyone else.

Handel last conducted *The Messiah* only eight days before he died in 1759. Part of *The Messiah* was played at his funeral. Near Handel's grave in Westminster Abbey is a statue of him holding a manuscript on which is written these words from *The Messiah*: "I know that my Redeemer liveth."

Its Spread Around the World and Shift to Christmastime
For the first two centuries it existed, Handel's *Messiah* was played annually at Easter, not at Christmas. It was not until partway through the 20th century that it gradually shifted to being performed more and more at Christmas and less and less at Easter. It has also undergone another transformation in some venues from that of a performance before an audience to one in which the audience members themselves participate.

 The Messiah was first heard in the U.S. on January 16, 1770, in the music room of the New York City Tavern.

🔔 *The Messiah* was performed by over 600 singers at London's Crystal Palace in 1834.

🔔 By the 1960s, Handel's *Messiah* had become almost exclusively associated with Christmas, and with that, its popularity grew.

🔔 Handel's *Messiah* is a popular choice as a charity fundraiser, and over the years audiences have given millions of dollars to help various causes. Better fundraising opportunities were the reason *The Messiah* shifted from being performed at Easter to at Christmas.

🔔 Since 1979, the San Francisco Conservatory of Music has organized an event called "Sing-It-Yourself Messiah." It is held in early December at the Davies Symphony Hall. Participants, often over 3000 of them, sing Handel's *Messiah*.

🔔 The original concept of having audience members sing Handel's *Messiah* was that of Martin Josman. It was done in New York City for the first time in 1967 and has since spread to other cities. Today, it occurs annually at Lincoln Center's Avery Fisher Hall.

The Nutcracker

The well-known Christmas ballet *The Nutcracker* is based on a story written by E.T.A. Hoffmann in 1819. The original choreographers of the ballet were Marius Petipa and Lev Ivanov. Pyotr Ilyich Tchaikovsky wrote the music. *The Nutcracker* was first performed on December 17, 1892, in St. Petersburg. It was not well received by the audience, who disliked that it had so many child performers as well as the grand music written by Tchaikovsky. It was not until 94-year-old William Christensen, working with George Balanchine, rewrote the ballet for children in 1954 that *The Nutcracker* became the Christmas hit that it remains today.

In *The Nutcracker*, a young girl named Clara Stahlbaum receives a Nutcracker figurine as a Christmas gift from her godfather Herr Drosselmeyer. Unfortunately, her brother Fritz accidentally breaks the Nutcracker and Clara is greatly upset. The children are sent to bed, but Clara sneaks back downstairs after all the guests have left. She magically shrinks to the size of the Nutcracker and other toys, including the toy soldiers her brother had received from Herr Drosselmeyer. Soon, the soldiers are attacked by mice. The Nutcracker quickly takes command of the soldiers. The Nutcracker and the King of the Mice battle each other. Clara's intervention allows the Nutcracker to defeat the Mouse King.

Turning into a prince, the Nutcracker takes Clara on a journey to the Kingdom of Sweets, where they are entertained by dancing snowflakes, flowers and sweet treats. The queen of the realm, called the Sugarplum Fairy, and the Nutcracker Prince perform a dance of gratitude for Clara. Some versions of the ballet end with Clara remaining in the Kingdom of Sweets while others have her return to her home in Nuremberg.

The Nutcracker is a hugely popular ballet, with many dance troupes auditioning young, upcoming dancers in the community to play the roles of Clara and Fritz. For some families, it is part of their yearly Christmas celebration. Indeed, it is so popular that many ballet troupes make the majority of their annual revenues from the performance of this ballet alone.

Fascinating Facts about *The Nutcracker*

The Nutcracker Suite is a concert piece by Tchaikovsky composed from eight pieces from the ballet: "Miniature Overture," "March," "Dance of the Sugarplum Fairy," "Russian Dance," "Arabian Dance," "Chinese Dance," "Dance of the Reed Flutes" and "Waltz of the Flowers." It should not be confused with the ballet.

In a 1919 production of *The Nutcracker* choreographed by Alexander Gorsky, the role of the Sugarplum Fairy was eliminated and Clara herself danced with the Nutcracker Prince.

The Nutcracker was first performed in its entirety outside of Russia in 1934.

Disney's animated movie *Fantasia* (1940) includes a segment from *The Nutcracker*.

Spike Jones and his City Slickers produced a version of *The Nutcracker* with lyrics in the 1940s.

In 1960, Duke Ellington and Billy Strayhorn took pieces of Tchaikovsky's music from *The Nutcracker* and rewrote them in jazz form.

In 1977, Nicaragua issued a set of 10 stamps commemorating *The Nutcracker*.

In *Beavis and Butthead's Christmas Special* (1995), Beavis compares the ballet's "Dance of the Sugarplum Fairy" to a heavy metal song.

In 1996, the Trans-Siberian Orchestra recorded a hard rock version of music from the ballet, entitling it "A Mad Russian's Christmas."

Pyotr Ilyich Tchaikovsky (1840–1893)

He composed his first song at the age of four.

His mother died from cholera when he was 14.

He studied law and became a civil servant.

He was a homosexual who had conflicted feelings about his sexual orientation. The romantic melodies of his overture *Romeo and Juliet* were inspired by his love for Eduard Zak.

He was part of a group of five composers known as "The Mighty Handful" or "The Five." The other four members of the group were César Cui (1835–1918), Modest Mussorgsky (1839–1881), Nicolai Rimsky-Korsakov (1844–1908) and Alexander Borodin (1833–1887).

His patron for 14 years was Nadeshda von Meck, who insisted that they never meet.

He married his student Antonina Milyukova when she threatened to commit suicide if he did not marry her. He fled married life within weeks and tried to kill himself.

He considered his sixth symphony, *The Pathètique*, his last work, also to be his best work.

He composed two other ballets: *Sleeping Beauty* and *Swan Lake*.

DID YOU KNOW?

Tchaikovsky's opera, *Vakula the Smith*, was based on Gogol's *Christmas Eve*. Rimsky-Korsakov also wrote an opera based on this same story.

Carol Symphony

In 1927, Victor Hely-Hutchinson wrote a unique piece of music that combined folk music, religious hymnody and classical music. The result was a choral prelude in four parts called the *Carol Symphony*. He based the first movement on the popular carol "O Come, All Ye Faithful." The second movement transitions into a prelude based on the traditional, secular carol "God Rest Ye Merry, Gentlemen." The third movement is based on a combination of two different carols—the medieval "The First Nowell" bookended by the equally old "Coventry Carol." The final movement returns to "O Come, All Ye Faithful," combining it this time with "Here We Come A-Wassailing." It was first performed in 1929.

A Ceremony of Carols

In 1942, composer Benjamin Britten (1913–1976) sailed on the Swedish ship *Axel Johnson* from New York City to England, stopping over in Halifax. There, he purchased a book called *The English Galaxy of Shorter Poems* by Gerald Bullett. This book inspired him to compose his well-known *Ceremony of Carols* during the remainder of his voyage. These are 11 medieval and early modern English and Scottish poems that Britten set to music.

 The processional and recessional are based on the Latin plainsong chant "Today Christ is Born."

🔔 After the processional is the 14th-century "Welcome Yule."

🔔 Then comes the 14th/15th-century "There is No Rose of Such Vertue."

🔔 That song is followed by "That Yonge Child" from the 14th century.

🔔 The 1567 Scottish ballad "Balulalow (or Cradle Song)" by the brothers James, John and Robert Wedderburn is next.

🔔 "As Dew in Aprille" (c. 1400) follows, comparing the unceremonius nature of Jesus' birth to the unassuming arrival of dew in the morning.

🔔 The militaristic work "This Little Babe" provides a contrast to the previous piece. It is an excerpt from the poem "New Heaven, New War" by the English poet Robert Southwell (died 1595).

🔔 A harp solo based on a plainsong simply entitled "Interlude" follows.

🔔 A piece based on another Robert Southwell poem, "In Freezing Winter Night," is next.

🔔 The poem "Spring Carol" by William Cornish (died 1523) celebrates the blessings God provides.

🔔 Finally, the 15th-century "Adam Lay I-Bounden" tells of how Adam's fall made necessary the birth of Christ.

DID YOU 🏠 KNOW?

Robert Southwell, the author of two poems used by Britten in *A Ceremony of Carols*, was a Catholic martyr. During the upheavals of the Reformation and counter-reformations of the

Church of England in the 16th century, Southwell was sent to the Continent to train to become a Jesuit priest. He returned to England to preach to those there who remained Catholic. Eventually he was captured and sentenced to death. He was hanged, drawn and quartered at Tyburn on February 21, 1595.

Amahl and the Night Visitors

In 1951, Gian Carlo Menotti (1911–2007) was commissioned by NBC Television to write and compose a one-act Christmas opera to be broadcast that December. It was the first opera written especially for television. Menotti used as his inspiration a painting by Hieronymus Bosch (died 1516) called "The Adoration of the Magi." The resulting opera, *Amahl and the Night Visitors*, was completed only a few days before the first performance/broadcast on December 24, 1951, at the NBC Opera Theatre in New York.

Amahl is a disabled boy with a penchant for telling tall tales. One evening when he comes in from playing outside, he tells his mother about a huge star he has seen in the night sky. His mother does not believe him. Later that night, there is a knock on the door. It is three kings—the Magi. They ask to rest there for the night, explaining that they are following a bright star to the birthplace of a great child. While the mother goes to fetch some wood, the kings show Amahl their gifts for the baby. Amahl tells them about how poor his family is and how his mother worries about his future. When his mother returns, Amahl goes to fetch some of the neighbors to help them entertain the kings. After everyone leaves and the kings are asleep, Amahl's mother attempts to steal some of the kings' gold but is caught. The kings offer to give her some gold but she declines in shame. Instead, she wishes to send a gift for the child but has nothing to give but Amahl's crutch. When Amahl and his mother offer the crutch to the kings for the Christ Child, Amahl's leg is miraculously healed. He journeys with the kings to see the baby Jesus and give him his crutch in thanksgiving.

🔔 The opera is short—only 48 minutes.

🔔 Menotti's wish was for Amahl always to be performed by a young boy.

🔔 Menotti was a musical prodigy who wrote the libretto and music for his first opera, *The Death of Pierrot*, at the tender age of 11.

🔔 Menotti was born and raised in Italy, spent his adult life in the U.S. and died in Monaco at the age of 95.

The Trans-Siberian Orchestra's Christmas Trilogy

The Trans-Siberian Orchestra is a hard rock/heavy metal band that incorporates classical, orchestral and progressive elements into its work. The group uses a full orchestra and uses choirs, as well. Guest singers and musicians often perform with the group. The composers and core members of the group are Paul O'Neill,

Robert Kinkel, Jon Olivia and Al Pitrelli. The group has produced three rock operas as part of a Christmas rock opera trilogy: *Christmas Eve and Other Stories* (1996), *The Christmas Attic* (1998) and *The Lost Christmas Eve* (2004).

Christmas Eve and Other Stories, the first of the rock opera trilogy, is about a young man who goes to a bar on Christmas Eve and encounters an old man who tells him a story about the special place Christmas Eve holds in the hearts and imaginations of many people. The opera contains both old and new tracks. "O Holy Night," "The First Nowell" and "God Rest Ye Merry, Gentlemen" are among the familiar tunes, while "A Star to Follow," "This Christmas Day" and the intriguing-sounding "A Mad Russian's Christmas" are new offerings.

The Christmas Attic, the second rock opera of the Christmas trilogy, also takes place on Christmas Eve. This time, an angel is sent down to earth to bring something to benefit humankind. The angel encounters a young girl who is confused about the meaning of Christmas. The two go up to the attic and open a large, old trunk. Inside, they discover many old Christmas cards and letters and set about reuniting old friends. In the process, the little girl discovers that love is the true meaning of Christmas, and the angel leaves the gift of love behind on earth. The song "The Ghost of Christmas Eve" speaks to the longing for connection and affection that all people feel. Another song included in the opera, "Christmas Canon," is a remake of John Pachelbel's "Canon in D Major" with lyrics added.

In the third and final rock opera of the Trans-Siberian Orchestra's Christmas trilogy, *The Lost Christmas Eve*, the same angel returns to earth to find the person who is most like Jesus. The angel encounters many people and follows the story of one man in particular—a man who disliked Christmas because his wife had died in childbirth on that day and his only son had been born brain damaged. After helping the father and son to reunite, the angel returns to heaven. He realizes that everyone is very much like Jesus at Christmastime. These travels into a Christmas past can be glimpsed in songs such as "Christmas Dreams," "Remember" and "What Child Is This?" Two other songs are remakes of classical works—Wolfgang Amadeus Mozart's "The Magic Flute" becomes "Queen of Winter Night," and Franz Liszt's "Hungarian Rhapsody No. 2" becomes "Wish Liszt (Toy Shop Madness)."

SONGS FOR THE SEASON OF GIVING

The Salvation Army

🔔 The Salvation Army began singing and playing Christmas carols in 1878.

🔔 Jay Livingston and Ray Evans, two Jewish songwriters, co-wrote "Silver Bells" for the 1951 Bob Hope movie *The Lemon Drop Kid*. They claimed to have been inspired by the sound of the Salvation Army bell ringers on the city street.

🔔 In the 1983 movie *A Christmas Story*, "Santa Claus Is Coming to Town" is played by the Salvation Army's Northeast Ohio Youth Band in a parade.

🔔 In 1987, Canadian singer Tom Jackson founded the Huron Carole Christmas concert fundraisers for the Salvation Army. These concerts raised over $3.5 million and continued until 2004, when they were replaced by another fundraiser featuring Jackson called Singing for Supper.

In Australia, the Myers stores sell a Christmas CD entitled *The Spirit of Christmas*. It is a compilation of recordings by various artists that changes every year. The proceeds of the sales are donated to the Salvation Army's Red Shield Appeal. This project began in 1993.

In 2011, singer Robert Davi released a new recording of "Mistletoe and Holly" in memory of Frank Sinatra, who had originally sung the song on his 1957 Christmas album. All proceeds from the sale of the single were donated to the 120th anniversary of the Salvation Army's Red Kettle Campaign.

DID YOU KNOW?

"Silver Bells" was originally called "Tinkle Bells" by composer Ray Evans. However, when his wife informed him that "tinkle" was a slang term for "urinate," he changed it.

Do They Know It's Christmas?

After watching a television special about the famine caused by the civil war in Ethiopia, Bob Geldof, leader of a minor Anglo-Irish band called the Boomtown Rats, got together with his friend Midge Ure, guitarist for the band Ultravox, and together they wrote "Do They Know It's Christmas?" about starving children in Africa. The single sold one million copies in the first week alone, jumping straight to number one on the charts.

Many individual artists and groups took part in recording the song, including Paul Young, Culture Club, Sting, Phil Collins, George Michael, Duran Duran, Paul McCartney, Spandau Ballet, Bananarama, members of U2, Ultravox, Status Quo,

Heaven 17, Kool and the Gang (the only American contributors) and others.

Sales of this single record raised £8 million in famine relief.

A Very Special Christmas

A Very Special Christmas is a series of Christmas music CDs with recordings by various artists. The proceeds from the sale of the CDs go toward helping fund the Special Olympics. Since the first volume was released, *A Very Special Christmas* has raised over US$100 million for the Special Olympics; the money helps fund athletic programs for intellectually disabled people around the world.

The first volume was originally put together by music producer Jimmy Iovine as a memorial compilation for his father; his wife Vicki suggested donating the funds to the Special Olympics. Volumes one through seven were released in 1987, 1992, 1997, 1999, 2001, 2003 and 2009. All the albums include selections from a wide variety of musical genres, except for volume six, which is primarily country and bluegrass. The same cover design has been used for every album. It features the Virgin Mary holding the infant Jesus. It was designed by Keith Haring. The series is produced by A&M Records.

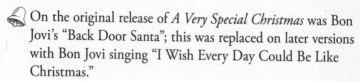 On the original release of *A Very Special Christmas* was Bon Jovi's "Back Door Santa"; this was replaced on later versions with Bon Jovi singing "I Wish Every Day Could Be Like Christmas."

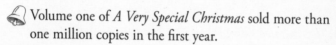 Volume one of *A Very Special Christmas* sold more than one million copies in the first year.

Chris Cornell and Eleven performed "Ave Maria" for *A Very Special Christmas* volume three. "Ave Maria" (or "Hail Mary") are the words the angel Gabriel uses to address the

Virgin Mary when he appears to tell her that she will give birth to the Son of God (Luke 1:28).

Also on volume three was "Children, Go Where I Send Thee," performed by Natalie Merchant. It is a traditional African American spiritual song. Each of the 12 numerical verses is given a meaning from the Bible.

A Very Special Christmas Live (1999) was recorded live at a benefit hosted by President Bill Clinton to celebrate the 30th anniversary of the Special Olympics.

The Killers' Christmas Singles for Product Red

In 2006, Product Red or (RED), a brand whose proceeds are dedicated to raising awareness and funds to help eliminate AIDS in Africa, was founded by U2 vocalist Bono (Paul David Hewson) and Bobby Shriver. Major companies can release products under the (RED) brand, and part of the proceeds from the sales go to charity. Many corporations participate, including Apple, Gap, Starbucks, Nike, Converse, American Express, Dell and Penguin.

Las Vegas alternative rock band the Killers has released a Christmas single every year since 2006 for the campaign— "A Great Big Sled" (2006), "Don't Shoot Me Santa" (2007), "Joseph, Better You than Me" (2008), "¡Happy Birthday Guadalupe!" (2009), "Boots" (2010) and "The Cowboys' Christmas Ball" (2011). In 2011, the group released all the songs on a CD entitled *The Killers' (RED) Christmas EP*. Musicians such as Elton John, Neil Tennant of the Pet Shop Boys and Mariachi El Bronx have collaborated with the Killers on these songs.

Matthew Gray Gubler, who plays FBI profiler Dr. Spencer Reid on the television series *Criminal Minds*, directed the music video for the Killers' second (RED) release, "Don't Shoot Me Santa."

The music video for "¡Happy Birthday Guadalupe!" starred Luke Perry, who played Dylan McKay on the former television series *Beverly Hills, 90210*.

The Killers' song "Boots" contains dialogue from the classic Christmas movie *It's a Wonderful Life* (1946). The opening of the "Boots" music video shows the death Charles Foster Kane, the fictional character from Orson Welles' 1941 film *Citizen Kane*, as he gazes at a snow globe. The video premiered on the Starbucks website on December 1—World AIDS Day—2010. Starbucks donated a nickel for every time the video was viewed.

The Killers' most recent Christmas single, "The Cowboys' Christmas Ball," has lyrics based on the 1890 poem of the same name by William Lawrence Chittenden (1862–1934).

SONGS THAT SELL

Christmas Carols and Capitalism

Not surprisingly, the capitalist economy of the Western World has harnessed Christmas carols and put them to use selling a variety of products. Some of these commercials use the song to link it and the good feelings associated with it to a particular product. Other commercials have rewritten the lyrics as a type of jingle. Here are just a few examples.

🔔 "It's the Most Wonderful Time of the Year" has been used in several back-to-school commercials by Staples, implying that it is when children return to school in September that is actually the most wonderful time of year for their parents. The song was written by Eddie Pola and George Wyle for singer Andy Williams' 1962 TV special, *The Andy Williams Christmas Show*, and featured on it in subsequent years. It was released on the singer's 1963 album, *The Andy Williams Christmas Album*.

🔔 One of the most successful television commercials to employ a Christmas song is one made to market Hershey's Kisses in 1996. The ad was so successful that it is still aired every Christmas season. The commercial features the chocolate treats in the form of a Christmas tree. The song "We Wish You a Merry Christmas" begins to play and the chocolate kisses function like bells accompanying the music. The commercial was designed by the New York City advertising agency Ogilvy and Mather and was directed by Carl Willat.

🔔 A 1998 Nintendo 64 holiday commercial used a parody of "Jingle Bells" to push the sale of video games to those who did not receive the ones they wanted for Christmas.

🔔 In 2005, Miller Lite Beer produced their "Enjoy the Lites" Christmas commercial in which the lights decorating a house were synchronized with the song "Wizards in Winter" by the Trans-Siberian Orchestra.

🔔 Walmart used "Carol of the Bells" in an ad in 2007.

🔔 A commercial promoting Apple's iPhone 3GS used new lyrics set to the traditional Christmas tune "The Twelve Days of Christmas." The gifts in the new lyrics were connected to 12 apps.

🔔 Tiffany & Co.'s 2010 Christmas commercial featured the song "Have Yourself a Merry Little Christmas."

🔔 The American indy duo Jack Conte and Nataly Dawn of Pomplamoose performed "Deck the Halls" in the 2010 Hyundai Genesis commercial.

🔔 Over the years, the Gap clothing company has produced holiday commercials featuring models dancing to various seasonal songs, including "Sleigh Ride," "I Saw Mommy Kissing Santa Claus" and "Jingle Bells."

Politicizing Christmas Carols

Everyone recognizes certain popular Christmas carols. Even if you do not celebrate the holiday, it is impossible to escape these songs in the malls and on the radio. Therefore, people—whether politicians or marketers—wanting to make a certain point and have it stick in people's minds have often used the catchy music of well-known carols. In the political realm, the Christmas lyrics are replaced with ones espousing the group's philosophy. Here are some examples from the past 250 years.

- During the French Revolution, French carols that listed the names of the three kings were altered by substituting the names of prominent revolutionary leaders.

- Some state songs are written to the tune of "O Christmas Tree," such as the previously mentioned songs of Maryland and Iowa (see p. 51), as well as "Delaware, My Delaware" and "Missouri, My Missouri."

- Following World War I, members of the growing Socialist movement rewrote many popular Christmas carols. The best-known was "Worker's Silent Night" by Bolesław Strzelewicz.

- Special carols were written for the period of Solidarity and martial law in Poland (1981–1982).

- In 2011, the lyrics of "Jingle Bells" were rewritten and sung by Filipino gays before Catholic bishops to protest the clergymen's opposition to proposed new anti-discrimination laws that would make it illegal to discriminate against a person based upon sexual orientation.

- In 2011, supporters of the Occupy Wall Street Movement sang Christmas songs with new lyrics that emphasized their message that most of the world's wealth is in the hands of very few and needs to be redistributed in a more equitable manner.

Flash Mob Caroling

Flash mob caroling is the newest trend in holiday singing in the Western World. A flash mob is a seemingly random event whereby a group of people suddenly converge on an area to perform some act, often a dance but in this case singing Christmas carols, and then disperse just as quickly. News of the gathering is spread through emails, text messages and online social media networks. On December 13, 2011, a flash mob caroling event at Algonquin College in Ottawa was directed by someone dressed as Darth Vader from *Star Wars*.

CAROLING AROUND THE WORLD

Christmas in Africa

🔔 In most of Africa, Christmas occurs during summer. It is common for people to carry candles while caroling.

🔔 In 1985, authorities in South Africa banned people in black and mixed-race communities from getting together to sing Christmas carols, saying that they constituted illegal gatherings. This was in the period when the struggles to end the apartheid in that country were intense.

🔔 In 1987, Gambia produced a set of 12 stamps, one for each verse of the "Twelve Days of Christmas."

🔔 In Ghana, groups of children go caroling in the early morning hours on Christmas. With their songs, they represent the angels bringing the good news of Jesus' birth. They often receive small treats from listeners.

🔔 A well-known Christmas carol in Madagascar is "Sambasamba Zanahary" ("It's a big opportunity Lord that you sent your only Son to save us from our sin").

In 1998, Tanzania issued various Rudolph, the Red-Nosed Reindeer stamps, including baby Rudolph, a head shot of Rudolph, Santa and Rudolph, as well as Rudolph balancing a ball on his nose.

In Kenya, carolers go about on Christmas Eve singing for money. These funds are then given to the local church.

In 2011, a group of South African musicians headed by singer and composer Boomtown Gundane recorded a response to Bob Geldof's 1984 Band Aid song "Do They Know It's Christmas?" Gundane said that some people were offended by Geldof's song, which he said implied that people in Africa were stupid as well as hungry. He said that proceeds from the sale of "Yes We Know It's Christmas" would go to fund instruction in contraception, discipline and literacy in British schools.

Carols by Candlelight: Australia

Unlike countries in the northern hemisphere, Christmas Day in Australia falls in the hottest part of summer. The Australian version of "Jingle Bells" reflects this fact: "Jingle bells, jingle bells, jingle all the way! / Christmas in Australia on a scorching summer's day, hey!" In this blistering heat, it just is not practical for people to go parading from door to door singing Christmas carols. So instead, the Aussies have created a Christmas caroling tradition of their own. It is called Carols by Candlelight, and it was first held in 1938.

Norman Banks, a radio announcer, was taking a walk during the Christmas holidays in 1937 when he noticed an old woman sitting alone. She was singing Christmas carols along with the radio in the soft glow provided by a single candle. Banks was moved by what he saw. It inspired him to organize a massive caroling event the next year.

Since then, Australians have gathered together on Christmas Eve in parks and stadiums to sing Christmas carols by the light of candles. At the larger gatherings, professional singers also perform. Some of these gatherings are huge, with up to 100,000 people. The largest such events take place in Sydney's Domain Gardens and Melbourne's Sidney Myer Music Bowl. The tradition has spread to nearby New Zealand.

The repertoire of songs includes many well-known Christmas carols sung throughout the world as well as a number of Aussie originals that reflect the unique holiday weather, traditions and wildlife of the country Down Under:

🔔 "Santa's Moving to the South Pole"

🔔 "Australians, Let Us Barbecue"

🔔 "The Australian Twelve Days of Christmas"

🔔 "The Three Drovers"

🔔 "The Melbourne Carol"

🔔 "Six White Boomers"

At midnight, the carolers join hands and sing "Auld Lang Syne."

Money raised at these events is given to charity. Several programs are broadcast on both radio and television so those who are unable to attend can still participate.

Bulgarian Koledari

Historically, Christmas Eve in Bulgaria was the time of the *Koleduvane*, a ritual blessing of people, animals and land through song. Though not as common now, it is still done in some areas.

The *koledari*, or carolers, are all men. They spend weeks preparing for this evening of song and neighborly goodwill. Costumes are prepared. The men wear hooded cloaks called *pamurluci*, embroidered white shirts, fancy leggings and sandals. On their heads, they wear fur hats called *kalpaci*, which are ornamented with wild flowers such as geraniums as well as boxwood. Each singer carries a carved wooden staff.

The men must learn and practice the many songs in the traditional repertoire, which consists of songs conveying blessings of prosperity and fertility on the various possible members of a household (the male and female heads of the household, seniors, children, unmarried women, etc.), as well as carols for the animals and the fields. There are also special songs that are performed when arriving at a house and when leaving it, and others for the walk in between houses.

At midnight on Christmas Eve, the carolers make their way from house to house. They are led by one of the older men, called the *stanenik*, who carries with him a cask of red wine and a cornel tree branch decorated with popcorn and pretzels. The singers themselves are divided into two groups according to age. When they perform, one group will sing a verse and then the other will repeat it.

When the men are done singing, they are presented with gifts of food: round buns called *koledni gevreci*, cheese-filled pastries known as *banisa*, plum or grape brandy called *rakia* as well as fruit, nuts, popcorn and other treats. Also, any unmarried girls will present a large bagel called a *kravai* to the leader of the group, the *stanenik*. He then holds it aloft and proclaims a blessing on the house.

On Christmas Day, after the singing is completed, the carolers divide up the food they have received. The men with a special sweetheart or an eye for a particular girl try to get the bagel that she baked. If more than one man wishes to receive a particular bagel, it is auctioned off to the highest bidder.

Chestita Koleda!

Canada Carols

Children in Canada used to sing carols door to door before World War II and in school Christmas concerts until just recently. Now, many schools feature only seasonal music and no longer allow the performing of religious music because of the vast array of religions practiced by their students. Today in Canada, not many people go caroling from door to door. Carolers are far more likely to be found performing at special events or in shopping malls. Some of these special events and old-time customs are listed below.

🔔 Some people of German descent have revived the old custom of "belsnicking" in Nova Scotia. People disguise themselves and go caroling on Christmas Eve. They continue singing and fooling around until their identities are guessed. Then everyone sits down together to celebrate the holidays.

🔔 Between Boxing Day and Epiphany in some areas of Newfoundland, people still participate in the old English caroling custom of "mummering." This is very similar to the German belsnicking, except that sometimes a play is also

performed. During the 1930s, mummering in Prince
Edward Island was called "lucky birding."

Since 1961, a Carol Ship, all decked out with lights and
a Christmas tree, has sailed in Vancouver Harbour every
evening the week before Christmas. It is often joined by several other boats. On board are children's choirs and bell
ringers whose music is broadcast to those gathered on shore.
Many of the onlookers join in the singing while gathered
around blazing bonfires to keep warm.

Since 1979, Calgary's St. Elizabeth of Hungary Church has
hosted the Stray Cats Party. This is a Christmas celebration
for those with nowhere else to go, such as homeless people,
new immigrants, refugees and some unemployed people.
The festivities conclude with the singing of "Silent Night,"
each person singing the internationally-known song in his or
her own language.

The CBC Radio program *As It Happens* hosts a Christmas
Eve special each year in which soldiers from Canadian
Armed Forces bases overseas are able to connect with their
families over the radio. The program includes a caroling por-
tion in which the soldiers at each base contribute a verse to
a well-known carol.

Caroling in the Caribbean

On Martinique, singers at Christmas feasts are accompanied
by "ti-bois." Basically, this means any two objects that a person can bang together.

In Trinidad, groups of singers go from house to house at
Christmas serenading the residents to the accompaniment of
cuatros and mandolins. This practice is called the "parang."

In the Dominican Republic, Christmas morning church
services include carols accompanied by accordians, guiras,

guitars, maracas and tambourines. Carolers also go singing from door to door.

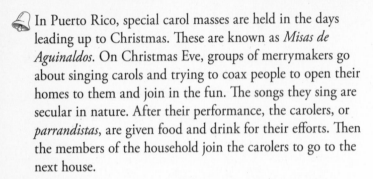

In Puerto Rico, special carol masses are held in the days leading up to Christmas. These are known as *Misas de Aguinaldos*. On Christmas Eve, groups of merrymakers go about singing carols and trying to coax people to open their homes to them and join in the fun. The songs they sing are secular in nature. After their performance, the carolers, or *parrandistas*, are given food and drink for their efforts. Then the members of the household join the carolers to go to the next house.

The Bahamas have featured many Christmas carols on their holiday stamps: "O Little Town of Bethlehem," "Little Donkey," "Silent Night" and "Hark! The Herald Angels Sing," all in 1988, and "While Shepherds Watched Their Flocks by Night," "We Three Kings," "Once in Royal David's City" and "I Saw Three Ships" in 2002.

Singing Christmas Carols in England

After the Reformation, caroling slowly died out in many parts of England, surviving mainly in the northern and western areas of the country. In the western counties, Christmas carols replaced psalms during the holiday church services. The old-English tradition of caroling was rescued and revived in the early 19th century by men like Sir John Stainer and John Mason Neale, who collected and published traditional songs. By the mid-19th century, Christmas carols were making a rapid comeback; caroling was very popular with the Victorians, and it was customary for guests and family members to gather around the piano to sing Christmas carols.

In medieval and early-modern England, carol singing began on St. Thomas' Day (December 21).

In many places in western England, it was customary to gather together in homes on Christmas Eve and sing carols from early evening until late into the night. This practice continued until the late 18th century.

In the city of Exeter, members of the various church choirs used to go caroling all night on Christmas Eve. They would gather at their church for service on Christmas morning where they would sing the "Old Hundreth Psalm" at the start of it.

At Adderbury, Oxfordshire, the village waits continued to sing during the Christmas holidays until the 1840s.

Carols were sung from the church tower at Condall, Hampshire, until about 1860.

At the Luttrell Arms in Dunster, Somerset, the traditional "Burning of the Ashen Faggot" occurs on Christmas Eve every year. In western England, a bundle of ash branches replaced the Yule log in people's fires. The bundle is tied with ashen "witheys"; each time one burned through, a toast was drunk and a carol sung.

After the Christmas Eve services on the Isle of Man, it was customary for the priest to depart, leaving the parishioners to their caroling. Each person sang a solo while holding a lit candle. If the candle went out, the person had to stop singing. By the 19th century, it had become traditional for the young maidens to mischievously pelt the young bachelors with peas while the songs were being sung.

On Britain's Scilly Islands, it was customary for church congregations to make monetary contributions to the church following carol singing at Christmastime.

In 19th-century Cornwall, the miners used to gather to sing carols in the mine shafts.

In Padstow, Cornwall, carolers go singing through the streets during the holiday season much as in many other towns. What makes the carolers of Padstow unique, however, is the songs they sing. Many of these songs are sung nowhere else. They have been handed down in families. Some are local versions of more well-known carols, such as "Harky, Harky," the Padstow version of "Hark! The Herald Angels Sing."

Gathering in the local pubs to sing Christmas carols is annual holiday tradition in the community of Dungworth in South Yorkshire. Every Sunday between Armistice Day in November and St. Stephen's Day in December, locals gather to sing songs of the season, songs that have been sung in the area for at least 200 years. Most of the songs are local tunes that are found only in the area of Dungworth—a few are even unique to a particular pub. Some, however, are more well known, such as "While Shepherds Watched Their Flocks by Night." Outsiders hearing the song may not recognize it immediately, though—it is sung to at least 25 different tunes in South Yorkshire (seven in Dungworth alone).

In 2011, members of Yorkshire's Pole Moor Riding Club and the Colne Valley Saddle Club went caroling on horseback. They were joined by many others walking with their dogs in "The Horsemen and Dog's Community Carol Service."

DID YOU KNOW?

Andy Park of Melksham, Wiltshire, England, began celebrating Christmas year-round in 1988 after his divorce. He leaves his decorations up and enjoys Christmas feasts every day. In June 1995, neighbors came by caroling. After they sang "Silent Night," Park treated them to some sherry.

Nine Lessons and Carols: An Anglican Christmas Tradition
The most popular Christmas program in English churches and on television is the Festival of Nine Lessons and Carols, based on Biblical readings from the Fall to the Reincarnation.

The original Nine Lessons and Carols was devised by Edward White Benson (1829–1896), Bishop of Truro, to fill in the void in the 1662 *Book of Common Prayer* for the newly rediscovered religious celebration of Christmas. Benson drew his inspiration for Nine Lessons and Carols from the practice of interspersing nine lessons throughout medieval feasts.

The King's College, Cambridge, version Nine Lessons and Carols was established in 1918. The readings from the Scriptures that come between the carols are delivered by representatives of the college, starting from the most junior and proceeding to the most senior. The carols featured in the annual festival vary from year to year except for the first one, which is always "Once in Royal David's City." An eight-year-old choir boy of King's College sings the first verse alone. All the boys learn the section, but not until that night do they discover who will get the honor of singing the solo.

The Fesitval of Nine Lessons and Carols at King's College, Cambridge, is extremely popular. The fact that attendance is free makes it even more so. People start lining up for the service up to three days in advance. For those who can't attend, Nine Lessons and Carols has been broadcast on radio every year since 1928, with the sole exception of 1930.

The Commissioned Carols of King's College, Cambridge
In 1982, Stephen Cleobury became the new Director of Music at King's College, Cambridge. In charge of the annual Nine Lessons and Carols service, Cleobury decided to incorporate more contemporary music into the program. He did this by holding a yearly contest from which a piece was selected to be performed at that year's concert. The first commissioned piece was Lennox Berkeley's "In Wintertime" in 1983, and there has been a new one every year since.

Caroling in Provence, France

In Provence, families would go out into the woods on Christmas Eve to cut down the Yule log and drag it back to their home. On their way back, they sang a carol in which they prayed for the Lord's blessings, asking him to make the women of the household, as well as the animals and the fields, fertile.

The most prolific and well-known writer of Provençal carols was the 17th-century priest Nicholas Saboly. Saboly wrote many Christmas carols, some of which are still sung in southern France today. Indeed, the songwriter's enduring popularity was evidenced in 1875 when a competition for a carol in the Provençal dialect was held on the bicentenary of his death.

In a unique carol from Provence, the Magi are depicted as gypsy fortune-tellers. In the song, they examine the hands of Jesus, Mary and Joseph and read their futures in the lines.

German Caroling Customs: Old and New

Quempas Singers

During the medieval period, everything had to be written out by hand; the printing press had not yet been invented. Choir members had to copy out the lyrics to hymns into booklets of their own. The carol "Whom of Old the Shepherds Praised" (*Quem Pastores Laudavere*) was popular and was often the first hymn to be copied. This led to these collections of hymns being known as Quempas books, a contraction of the first words of the carol.

It was during this same period that groups of poor scholars would go from house to house during the holiday season singing Christmas carols in the hope of receiving a gift in return. These singers took their name from the popular carol mentioned above and were known as the Quempas singers. In some areas of Saxony and Thuringia, Quempas singers are still found, though they are not necessarily students. In Bavaria, they go caroling on Epiphany.

Tower Singers

Another customary caroling practice in Germany that still survives in a few towns to this day is that of tower singing. Carols are sung from the tower of the local church, sometimes to the accompaniment of a trumpet. Martin Luther's most well-known carol, "From Heaven Above to Earth I Come," is frequently sung.

Thuringian Customs

On Christmas Eve, peasants in Thuringia form a torchlight procession that goes up to the top of a hill where a pyramid of stones has been built. They walk around the pyramid a few times singing Christmas carols before tossing their torches on the pyramid. Then they march back to town, singing by candlelight.

CAROLING AROUND THE WORLD

At midnight on Christmas Eve, the bells are rung in churches in Thuringia. This is followed by the villagers gathering to sing a carol. Then, the bells are rung again and another song is sung. This sequence is repeated a third time before being completed with a dance.

Star Singers

The custom known as "star singing" is widespread in Europe and dates back centuries. Star singers go from door to door during the holidays not only in Germany but also in Sweden, Norway, Denmark, Poland, Ukraine, Russia, Romania and the Netherlands (where the tradition goes back to at least the 18th century).

In Poland, this form of caroling was known as *gwiazdory* ("caroling with a star"). In rural areas of Poland, the lead caroler carried a star on a pole. Another singer was dressed as King Herod. The rest were attired as shepherds and angels. Another group of carolers went about on the Feast of the Three Kings (Epiphany) dressed as the three Wise Men, with one even blackening his face with soot. The leader carried a lantern shaped like a star. These Star Boy carolers would sing a song in front of a house. If invited in, they would sing more songs, both religious and secular, inside.

In neighboring Ukraine, carolers are also led by a person carrying a star. One person is dressed like a goat. Many of the other singers carry and play simple instruments. At each house, they sing a song for every member of the household. They then perform a short skit involving the death and resurrection of the goat. This is likely some strange amalgamation of an ancient fertility rite with the death and resurrection of Christ. The carolers generally receive a few coins for their efforts.

🔔 In Russia, the star or lantern carried by the singers is frequently constructed out of pasteboard. It has a transparent center with an image of the baby Jesus.

🔔 In Romania, the star is made of wood and the pictures include the Nativity, Adam and Eve, and angels. It is decorated with bells.

🔔 In Switzerland, there are groups of carolers known as *Sternsinger* ("star singers"). They proceed through town carrying stars and singing. They are accompanied by the characters from the story of Jesus' birth.

🔔 In Germany, star singing took on a variety of regional customs. For example, in Usethal the star singers performed on Christmas Eve, while in Upper Innthal it was on Epiphany Eve. In the Tyrol, the singers used to stamp about the fields near a farmer's house to encourage a good crop in the coming year.

Star singers were common in Germany until the end of the 19th century, when the church authorities began to frown upon it, feeling it had become too secularized. This led to the custom dying out in many regions. However, the custom was revived following the end of World War II. Numerous new Christmas songs were created, and star singers began collecting money for missionaries overseas. In the past generation, girls started to join the boys at star singing, even though it is still only the boys who dress as the Magi.

Fröliche Weinachten!

Greece: Different Carols for Different Occasions

Children in Greece go caroling on Christmas Eve, New Year's Eve and Epiphany Eve. Each night has its own set of songs celebrating the occasion: the birth of Jesus, the New Year and St. Basil, and the baptism of Jesus. The carols follow a standard format. The first section is about the cause of the celebration; the second wishes the members of the household well; and the third requests a token of appreciation for the singers.

Families attend Midnight Mass on Christmas Eve. Families walk to the church preceded by boys who bang on drums and sing carols. They are often given treats, such as candy, nuts and figs, for their efforts. A few hours later, when dawn is breaking, Greek children go caroling once more, keeping time to the singing with triangles and drums.

Carolers on St. Basil's Day (January 1) carry hollow ships made of wood, metal or cardboard. People throw coins and treats into the ships in gratitude for the carolers' songs. The ships represent the one in which St. Basil is believed to sail to Greece to deliver presents to children on New Year's Day.

The vast majority of Greek carols have the same meter, so the music is interchangeable. The oldest-known Greek carol is the medieval "Byzantine Carol" (or "God Who Has No Beginning Descended"). There are many local Greek carols, such as the Peloponnesian "Christmas, Firstmas."

The Greek Island of Chios

On the island of Chios in the 19th century, Christmas was much like modern-day Halloween. On the day before Christmas, children went door to door singing carols and carrying baskets to hold the treats they received.

Then on Christmas Day, the priest, deacons and candle-lighters of each parish processed from house to house singing carols and collecting alms. Each man had a job—one played the lyre, a second the harp, a third the cymbals, and a fourth chanted the lyrics. The fifth man led the rest with a lit candle. He would inquire at each house before the musicians arrived if there was any reason, such as death or illness, that made it inappropriate for them to sing. If it was fine, they would sing a carol and be invited in for a drink and food. Then they would sing playful carols appropriate to the household—for example, a lover's song for a couple engaged to be married. The inhabitants of the house gave donations to the church at the conclusion of the caroling.

Kala Christouogena!

Piping Away Mary's Pain: Italy

Zampogna is the name given to a type of bagpipe played in Italy. It has two pipes and a bag that was traditionally made from the hide of a goat. The men who play this instrument are known as *zampognari.*

In the days and weeks leading up to Christmas, shepherds used to come down to the towns and play songs in front of the shrines to the Virgin Mary. There were usually two men, one playing the zampogna and the other the ciaramella (a type of flute). The songs were meant to ease Mary's birthing pains. The zampognari also played before the homes of carpenters in honor of Mary's husband Joseph, who was himself a carpenter. In the past, the townspeople would reward the efforts of the zampognari with gifts of food.

Today, the zampognari are rarely shepherds but rather men from the towns and cities who pipe to keep a tradition alive. The zampognari can be heard at Christmastime in Rome, Abruzzo, Molise, Lazio, Sicily, Campania, Basilicata and Calabria. Most household manger scenes in Italy include a shepherd playing the zampogna. Over the two days before Christmas, children in Italy dress as shepherds and go about serenading people on shepherd's pipes. They also sing songs and recite poems.

"From Starry Skies Descending" is a popular Christmas song in Italy. The music and lyrics were written by St. Alphonsus Maria de Liguori (1696–1787), founder of the Redemptorist Order. He based this song on the well-known zampognari tune "When the Child was Born," also known as "Carol of the Bagpipers." This song is believed to have originated in Sicily in the 17th century.

Filipinos Sing in the Season

Christianity and the celebration of Christ's birth were introduced to the people of the Philippines by Spanish colonists and Catholic missionaries in the 16th century. In the Philippines today, Christmas celebrations begin nine days prior to the 25th of December. This period is known as Simbang Gabi. Early morning mass is held and carolers are numerous in the evenings. The carolers go about between six o'clock and midnight each night.

In some parts of the country, carolers wear folk costumes and are accompanied by people on guitars and with castanets. A traditional ring dance is performed. Scenes from Jesus' birth are re-enacted. Both carols and traditional folk songs are sung.

Carolers are especially numerous in the few hours leading up to Midnight Mass on Christmas Eve. Banjos accompany the singers. Carolers always receive tokens of appreciation for their singing, but on Christmas Eve they are often given more. Families then walk to Midnight Mass, often singing Christmas carols.

Carolers in the Philippines usually end their performances with the singing of "Maligayang Pasko" to the tune of "Happy Birthday." The two most popular English carols in the Philippines are "Jingle Bells" and "White Christmas." In 2011, Catholic Monsignor Pedro Quitorio urged carolers in the Philippines to return to singing the traditional *panunuluyan* or *panarit* Bible verses of the Nativity story because it is both catechetical and allows audience participation.

The Many Caroling Customs of the Poles

The Polish people have a great number of caroling traditions. Singing Christmas songs, both religious and secular, was an important part of the Christmas festivities and took place at church, at home and going from door to door. Caroling generally took place from Christmas Day to Candlemas (February 2).

On Christmas Day in Poland, families used to gather around the hearth to sing Christmas hymns and songs. On the morning of December 26, a child would enter each house in the village to wish the inhabitants well and to sing about Jesus' birth. On New Year's Day, the local priest and his assistants went caroling door to door.

The Polish caroling custom known as *turoń* dates back to at least the 16th century. It takes its name from the wild ox (or *tur*). One of the participants was required to dress as an animal and walk on all fours. He would be led on a leash by another caroler. This caroler might dress as a beggar, a Turk or a Jew (Jews and Muslim Turks representing the two closest opposing religions). The group would sing a song outside a house. After being invited in, the *turoń* would get up to all sorts of silly antics until finally the members of the household would sing a song asking the *turoń* to leave. The carolers would be given a treat or some coins for their efforts. *Turoń* caroling occurred between Christmas Eve and Epiphany.

"Herody" was a form of Christmas entertainment in Poland that combined acting with caroling. The participants were young men aged between 16 and 20. One man dressed as King Herod. The others dressed as a variety of characters depending on their number and available costumes—for example, Herod's general, a soldier, an angel, the Wise Men, the Devil, Death, a Turk or a Jew. The men would ring a bell and sing a carol in front of a house. When the door opened, they would ask permission to enter. Once inside, they would perform a play about the killing of the Holy Innocents, concluding with another carol. After some refreshments, the group would proceed to the next house.

The Polish tradition of caroling with a *szopka* (manger) developed in the early 18th century. A group of usually three boys went door to door carrying a manger scene with puppet characters they had made. The characters, however, were not the Holy Family but King Herod, the Wise Men, an angel, a soldier and perhaps others. Two of the boys carried the *szopka* while the third hid behind it and manipulated the puppets. Through songs, the boys told the tale of King Herod's killing of all boys under two in his attempt to kill Jesus.

In Poland, the Feast of the Three Kings (Epiphany) was called *szczodry wieczór*, meaning "bountiful or plentiful evening." Families sang Christmas songs around the hearth. Poor children went caroling. In return for their efforts, they received a wheat bread called *szczordraki* baked especially for this purpose. Some of their songs even mentioned this treat.

Wesołych Świąt!

DID YOU KNOW?

Part of Pope John Paul II's first Christmas celebration as Pope in 1978 included the singing of carols, one of which came from his native Poland, by 50,000 schoolchildren of Rome.

Q: What nationality is Santa?

A: North Pole-ish!

Singing in the Yule in Scandinavia

"Blowing in the Yule" is a tradition in German and Scandinavian areas of Europe. A group of musicians with their instruments go up into the local church tower. There, they play four Christmas carols, one in each direction. Afterward they ring the church bells, announcing to the community that Christmas has arrived. This practice has its roots in the pagan (and later Christian) belief that loud sounds would keep evil beings away.

Julotta is a church service that takes place on Christmas morning in Lutheran churches in Scandinavia. This service consists mainly of carol singing.

Singing Christmas carols in the home on Christmas Eve is a common practice throughout the Scandinavian countries. In Denmark, people join hands in a circle around the Christmas tree after dinner on Christmas Eve. They sing carols as they walk around it. In Norway, they also gather around the tree to sing carols. Most of these carols include accompanying gestures and actions. On Christmas Eve in Sweden, family members join hands around the Christmas tree. They dance around the tree and throughout the house singing "Now It Is Christmas Again" (*Nu är det Jul igen*).

Carolers also go from door to door singing. A 2000 Finnish Christmas stamp depicted costumed *Tiernapojat* carol singers.

A number of Christmas songs that were written by Englishmen in the 19th century were set to music found in a collection known as *Piae Cantiones* ("Devout Songs"). These were compiled by a Finnish cleric and schoolmaster named Jaakko Suomalainen in 1582.

Glad Jul (Swedish)

Gledelig Jul (Norwegian and Danish)

Hauskaa Joulua (Finnish)

DID YOU  KNOW?

In 2000, Sweden chose Christmas carols for depiction on its stamps. The songs chosen were all national in character—"Now It Is Christmas Again," "Three Gingerbread Men," "The Fox Runs over the Ice" and "Christmas Has Come to Our House."

Spanish Villancicos

On Christmas morning in Spain, the family gathers around their manger scene (something most families living in southern Europe have in their homes rather than a Christmas tree). A figurine of the baby Jesus is placed in the manger. Then the children of the family entertain their elders by dressing up as peasants and singing villancicos while playing along on tambourines and castanets. Later, everyone joins in the singing.

A *villancico* was a term originally applied to Spanish folk songs in general, but now refers specifically to those about the Nativity. The term *villancico* was derived from the word *villano*, meaning "shepherd." Many of these songs were likely composed by lonely shepherds as a means of passing the time during the long days and nights spent guarding their flocks in the fields.

The first generations of Catholic clerics and nuns in Spain's New World Empire wrote numerous Christmas villancicos that have survived to this day; some forgotten in dusty archival manuscripts, others well known and heard in churches and homes each holiday season.

- Gaspar Fernandes (c. 1566–1629), organist and chapel master at Antigua Guatemala Cathedral, composed 80 Christmas villancicos for the local populace between 1609 and 1620.

- Juan Gutiérrez de Padilla (c. 1590–1664), organist at Puebla Cathedral in Mexico, wrote several Christmas villancicos for the congregation there.

- Sr. Juana (1651–1695), the most well-known early Mexican poet, wrote many Christmas villancicos that are still in print today.

Riu, Riu, Chiu

"Riu, Riu, Chiu" is a Spanish villancico from the 16th century that is still sung today. The phrase "riu, riu, chiu" comprises nonsense words meant to imitate the sounds of a nightingale. This villancico from Catholic Spain tells of how Mary was born without sin so that she could be the mother of Christ. It was published in Venice in 1556 in a work entitled *Cancionero de Uppsala* ("Songs of Uppsala"). It has been recorded by several modern artists, including The Monkees, who sang it on their Christmas television special in 1967.

Los Pastores

Los Pastores is a Spanish folk play that dates back to the Middle Ages. It tells the story of Jesus' birth from the viewpoint of the shepherds who set out to see Him in his manger bed. This traditional Christmas play was taken by Spanish colonists to many areas of the world and is popular in Mexico and the American Southwest. At the end of the performance, the cast and the audience join together to sing "Silent Night."

DID YOU KNOW?

The earliest reference to caroling in the New World comes from the archives of Mexico City's cathedral. There, in 1538, a canon was paid to train the choir boys to sing Christmas villancicos in the church services on Christmas Eve and Christmas Day.

Singing in the Season in Switzerland

The Fountain Singers of Rheinfelden

Since 1541, 12 members of the Brotherhood of St. Sebastian from the town of Rheinfelden have gathered on Christmas Eve to take part in a local custom called *Brunnensinger* ("fountain singing"). The men dress in black and wear tall black hats. They walk from fountain to fountain, stopping to sing a carol at each of the seven fountains. Every time God or Christ is mentioned in the carol, the singers remove their tall hats. The procession and singing is in remembrance of those people who died in the horrendous bubonic plague year of 1348.

The Christmas Rose Watch

In Poschiviavino, an ancient custom known as the "Christmas rose watch" is still kept. The Christmas rose is a type of rose of Jericho from the Arabian Peninsula. When the conditions are dry, the plant wilts into a compact bundle. It is this bundle that the Swiss women place in a bowl of water on a table. The women then join in singing carols until the rose "blooms" again.

Advent Caroling

In the German-speaking areas of Switzerland in the north, east and central regions of the country, families hang Advent wreaths with four candles. Families light a new candle each Sunday during Advent and then sing carols together.

Before the beginning of Advent, people in Switzerland receive a caroling booklet in the mail. It is sent annually from Swiss Radio. With this booklet, anyone who wishes may join in with the people singing carols over the radio every Sunday in the Advent season. Those who prefer may go to the radio station and be part of the group of singers whose voices are being broadcast over the airwaves.

Seasonal Singing in Ukraine

Ukrainians have a long history of singing at Christmastime. Nestor the Chronicler, who recorded the life and times of St. Vladimir the Great, Prince of Kiev (980–1015), wrote about the Ukrainian people gathering to sing songs about Christ's birth during the Christmas season. However, this tradition even pre-dates the acceptance of Christianity among the Ukrainians in the year 988. These pre-Christian carols tell about the creation of the world as well as about historic people and events.

In Ukraine, Christmas carols are called *koliadky*. The name derives from Koliada, a pagan goddess of the sun and sky. Her festival was between January 6 (Epiphany) and 19. Many traditions relating to these celebrations were later merged with Christianity. In fact, many traditional Ukrainian *koliadky* are not even about the birth of Christ or Christmas festivities. Romance is actually a very popular theme of these songs—love, courtship and marriage.

In Ukraine, *koliadky* are sung between Christmas Day and New Year's Eve. Carolers always stop at the house of the local priest first. In eastern Ukraine, caroling groups are made up of young people and children. In western Ukraine, in the Hutsul region of the Carpathian Mountains, carols are sung by groups of men called *tabory*. The leader of the group carries a cross. The other men each carry an ax decorated with bells. The men proceed from house to house dancing a special hopping dance and singing songs called *pliasaky*. At each house, they stop and bow three times. Then the leader sings a song with the other men joining in on the refrain. All the time, they are ringing the bells on their axes and stomping their feet.

Between New Year's Day and Epiphany, another type of carol is sung in Ukraine. These carols are known as *shchedrivky* ("Epiphany songs").

Unique to the United States

Americans were late-comers to the practice of singing Christmas carols. The Puritans who settled the country were opponents of the celebration of Christmas and outlawed it. Those who attempted to celebrate Christmas between 1659 and 1681 found themselves having to pay a fine. For decades, the House of Representatives met on December 25 just as on any other day. Indeed, Christmas was not made a federal holiday in the United States until 1870. Nonetheless, once Americans embraced the holiday, the festivities surrounding it became immense. Today, Christmas is the most profitable time of the year for retailers, who sell Christmas gifts, decorations and, of course, music.

Before the American Civil War and the end of slavery in the U.S., black slave men would dress up on Christmas Eve in colorful rags and masks. They would make music with whatever was available—bones, horns, Jew's harps. Known as John Kuners, these men went from house to house on the plantation, beginning with the main house and ending at their quarters, singing Christmas songs. They were often rewarded for their effort with a few pennies.

John Wanamaker opened his Philadelphia department store in 1911. It contained a big open area called the Grand Court. In it was the world's largest pipe organ. At Christmas, Wanamaker had the Grand Court transformed into a cathedral. The store's musical director led twice-daily carol and hymn sing-a-longs during the holiday season. Soon, the store was printing its own annual Christmas hymnal for its customers—a practice that continued into the 1950s. The hymnal contained a variety of Christmas songs, but religious ones made up the largest number.

In Atlanta, Rich's Department Store used to mark the season with choir singing and a tree-lighting ceremony. This tradition first occurred in 1948 and continued until the store became part of Macy's in 2003.

Lou Hoover, wife of President Herbert Hoover (in office 1929–1933), liked to turn off all the lights in the White House and then go caroling from room to room with her family, using candles to light their way.

An early custom at New York City's Barnard College was for members of the graduating class to dress in their academic robes and go about the dormitories singing Christmas carols to their fellow students.

During the 1950s, Saks Fifth Avenue in New York placed life-size paper-maché carolers in niches above its windows. Pipe organs were placed above them. Carols sung by employees were played.

At the annual lighting of the Washington Square Christmas tree in New York, people gather to sing Christmas carols along with a brass band.

For the annual Christmas show, each of the 140 cast members of the Radio City Music Hall dresses in a Santa costume to sing "Here Comes Santa Claus."

There are hours of pre-lighting singing performances by well-known artists before the annual lighting of the Rockefeller Christmas tree in New York City. In 2011, the line-up included Kylie Minogue singing "Santa Baby" and Josh Groban performing "The Christmas Song."

Liberace used to set up very elaborate and expensive Christmas displays in his yard in Sherman Oaks, California. Speakers blasting Liberace singing Christmas songs were part of the display.

Since 1998, Tennessee court judge Tom Dubois has been giving those convicted of speeding during the Christmas holidays the option of paying their fine by singing a Christmas song to the court.

Every year on Christmas Eve in Philadelphia, people gather around a tall decorated spruce tree known as the Children's Christmas Tree, which grows in Independence Square, to sing Christmas carols.

In Phoenix, Arizona, carol singers with homemade paper lanterns hike up Squaw Peak to sing carols on the top.

Each year, carolers sing underground in Kentucky's Mammoth Cave, part of the largest-known tunnel system in the world.

The business community in Austin, Texas, uses the carol the "Twelve Days of Christmas" to present its annual Twelve Nights of a Capital Christmas. Among the festivities is an egg hunt at the Austin Crest Hotel on the sixth day—"six geese a-laying"—and a Scottish ball complete with bagpipes on the eleventh night—"eleven pipers piping."

At Disney's Epcot Center in Florida, a grand "Holidays Around the World" celebration is held. It includes music by a 50-piece orchestra and a 450-voice choir along with hundreds of carolers marching in a candlelight procession. The Christmas story is told by a visiting celebrity.

In the past few decades, the celebration of Christmas as a Christian holiday has been highly controversial in the U.S. as the religious make-up of the country has become more diverse and fewer people are practicing any religion at all. Many court cases have challenged the singing of religious holiday songs in schools and the display of the Nativity scene on government property. In some places, such activities are no longer allowed. In December 2011, the post office manager in Silver Springs, Maryland, evicted a group of carolers from the premises, stating that the singing of Christmas carols was not allowed on government property.

DID YOU KNOW?

When Ozella McHargue of St. John, Indiana, died in 2004, her family gave this Christmas-loving lady a holiday-themed funeral, complete with Christmas carols rather than the more traditional funeral music.

The Caped Carolers of Glen Rock

A year before the gold rush of 1849, five men who had recently settled in the new community of Glen Rock in California decided to get together at Christmastime to keep up the tradition of going house to house singing carols that they had practiced back home in the English counties of Cheshire, Derbyshire and Yorkshire. These five men—George Shaw, Mark Radcliffe and Charles, Mark and James Heathcote—originally had a repertoire of only four songs—"Christmas Hymn," "Hark Hark," "While Shepherds Watched Their Flocks by Night" and "Hosanna"—all of which they had learned back home in England.

Over the years, other men joined these five, bringing new songs with them. Today, the Glen Rock Carolers is comprised of 50 singers, each of whom has had to serve an apprenticeship with a member and wait until a spot became vacant before he could join the group. The group's increased musical selection includes

"Ye Faithful," "Glory to God," "Softly Sweetly," "O Christmas Tree," "Silent Night," "O Jesus Star of the Morning," "When Christ was Born" and "Raise Christians, Raise." Each of the songs is performed in three-part harmony.

Since 1934, the group has worn costumes while caroling. These outfits have changed over the years. Today, members wear a gray woolen tweed coat with a gray hat and gloves. Each member wears a woolen scarf in a color of his own choosing. Each man also carries a black cane. While they process through the community singing carols, the group is led by the Peanut Man, who hands out peanuts to listeners, and a Torch Bearer, who carries a lantern to light the way. The group also once had a Dog Pelter, whose duty was to keep dogs away from the carolers; however, it is no longer necessary to have anyone do this.

St. Louis Christmas Carols Association

In 1911, William Danforth (1870–1955) and a group of his friends began an annual tradition of going caroling in their city of St. Louis. The coins that the group received as tokens of appreciation from the houses at which they sang were donated to a local charity, the Children's Aid Society. Members have donated their proceeds to various charitable causes over the past century. In 2011, two carols—"Carol of the Holy Child" and "Caroling in St. Louis"—were written especially for the St. Louis Christmas Carols Association to commemorate their 100th anniversary.

Venezuela: The Gift of Song

In Venezuela, the lead-up to Christmas is celebrated with a series of nine early-morning (4:30 AM) masses. These begin on December 16 and, despite the early hour, are well attended; most people attend at least one. Of course, it is difficult to remain asleep when the call to church is signaled by bells ringing and firecrackers exploding.

In Venezuela, the term for a Christmas song or carol is *aguinaldo*, and these early-morning church services before Christmas are called the *Misas de Aguinaldo*. As in several Slavic languages, the term used for carol is also the term used to describe a gift. Thus, these carols are seen as gifts, both for Jesus and for the listeners.

In Caracas, the capital of Venezuela, a unique tradition is observed. Many people, mainly youths, roller-skate to these early-morning services. Vehicles are not allowed on the roads before 8:00 AM to keep everyone safe. Children tie a string around one of their toes before going to bed and leave the end of the string dangling out their bedroom windows. If they sleep in, someone roller-skating past will yank on the string to wake them.

Christmas carols are sung both at these nine masses and out in the streets. While not so common anymore, some groups of young men still go from house to house singing carols. They accompany themselves on folk instruments, such as the *furruco* (a small drum with a stick in the middle), the *cuatro* (a small, four-string guitar) and *maracas* (rattles). When these young men end up serenading a group of young women, the songs often shift from Christmas carols to love songs.

The importance of music to Christmas celebrations in Venezuela is attested to by the series of holiday stamps the government issued in 1996: out of 10 stamps, four are pictures of groups of musicians singing.

Christmas Caroling in Wales

Plygain

A pre-dawn church service used to be held in Wales on Christmas morning. It was known as "plygain," deriving from the Latin *pulli cantus* or "cock crow song." The evening before was spent with family and friends singing Christmas songs and generally making merry. Families have their own special carols that they sing at plygain. More singing occurred during the services, which largely consisted of singing carols. The church itself was lit by special plygain candles for the service. This tradition survived the Protestant Reformation of the 15th and 16th centuries, being continued by both the Anglican and later the Methodist churches. Today, the custom is practiced mainly in central Wales.

Star of Bethlehem

A former Welsh caroling custom among the colliers involved carrying candles, either attached to a board or stuck into a wheelbarrow full of clay, from house to house. Called the Star of Bethlehem, this candlelit contraption was set before each house while the men kneeled and sang a Christmas carol. They usually received some token of gratitude in return.

Eisteddfod

An annual Christmas event in Wales is the "eisteddfod." This is a carol and poetry writing contest. Christmas must be the subject of the poem. Later, the winning poem is set to music by choirs across Wales who then perform in market squares throughout the country, vying for the honor of having their tune designated the official one. Winning songs from former years are also sung.

Nadolig Llawen!

More Caroling Around the World

In Armenia, children climb up onto the rooftops to sing Christmas carols. Later, adults fill their handkerchiefs with coins and raisins.

On Christmas Eve in Austria, groups of carolers go from house to house carrying a manger scene and singing.

The Bhil people of northwestern India are Christians who go about singing Christmas hymns every night for a week at Christmastime.

In Ireland, carolers perform for shoppers in the market areas across the country. Any money collected is donated to charity.

Macedonians use the old Julian calendar, so they celebrate Christmas on January 6. On Christmas morning, men go from house to house singing a special carol wishing everyone well.

Christians in Malaysia have to obtain a police permit to sing Christmas carols in church or in their home.

December 26 is the great day of caroling in the Netherlands. Choirs and professional music groups perform everywhere. Carol programs are broadcast on the radio and television.

In the days leading up to Christmas, carolers in Romania go door to door singing songs wishing people good fortune in the future.

At Midnight Mass on Christmas Eve, members of the Russian Orthodox Church gather in the church to sing Christmas hymns after making a procession around the outside of the building led by a priest holding a cross aloft.

Early on Christmas morning before mass, Serbian children go around banging on doors and singing silly songs. They are rewarded with nuts, candy and coins.

On Epiphany, Slovakian children go door to door in groups of three, dressed in white robes with crosses around their necks. They sing in return for alms.

Sing, sing the joyful song,
Let it never cease,
Of glory in the highest,
On earth, good will and peace.
—from "Sing, Sing for Christmas" by J.H. Edgar

CHRISTMAS CAROLS IN THE PUBLIC DOMAIN

Adeste Fideles

Words and music: John Francis Wade (1711–1786)

1. Adeste Fideles laeti triumphantes,
Veníte, veníte in Bethlehem.
Natum vidéte, Regem Angelorum:

Veníte adoremus,
Veníte adoremus
Veníte adoremus Dóminum

Angels We Have Heard on High

Words: traditional French carol; translated by Bishop James
Chadwick (1813–1882)

1. Angels we have heard on high
Sweetly singing o'er the plains,
And the mountains in reply
Echoing their joyous strains.

Refrain
Gloria, in excelsis Deo!
Gloria, in excelsis Deo!

Away in a Manger

Words: verses 1 & 2, unknown, 1885; verse 3, attributed to
John Thomas McFarland (1851–1913)

1. Away in a manger, no crib for His bed,
The little Lord Jesus laid down His sweet head;
The stars in the sky looked down where He lay,
The little Lord Jesus, asleep in the hay.

2. The cattle are lowing, the poor Baby wakes.
But little Lord Jesus, no crying He makes.
I love Thee, Lord Jesus, look down from the sky.
And stay by the cradle till morning is nigh.

3. Be near me, Lord Jesus, I ask Thee to stay,
Close by me forever, and love me, I pray!
Bless all the dear children in Thy tender care
And take us to heaven, to Live with Thee there.

Bring a Torch, Jeanette, Isabella

Words and music: French Provençal carol by Émile Blémont;
translated by Edward Cuthbert Nunn (1868–1914)

1. Bring a torch, Jeanette, Isabella
Bring a torch, to the cradle run!
It is Jesus, good folk of the village;
Christ is born and Mary's calling;
Ah! ah! beautiful is the Mother
Ah! ah! beautiful is her Son!

Carol of the Beasts

Words: traditional

1. Jesus our brother, kind and good
Was humbly born in a stable rude
And the friendly beasts around Him stood,
Jesus our brother, kind and good.

Coventry Carol

Words: attributed to Robert Croo, 1534

1. Lullay, Thou little tiny Child,
By, by, lully, lullay.
Lullay, Thou little tiny Child.
By, by, lully, lullay.

Deck the Halls

Words: Welch lyrics "Nos Galan" by Talhaiarn (John Jones, 1810–1869); translated by Thomas Oliphant (1799–1873)

1. Deck the halls with boughs of holly,
Fa la la la la, la la la la,
'Tis the season to be jolly,
Fa la la la la, la la la la,
Fill the mead-cup, drain the barrel,
Fa la la, la la, la la la,
Troul the ancient Christmas carol,
Fa la la la la, la la la la.

Ding Dong Merrily on High

Words: George Ratcliffe Woodward (1848–1934)

1. Ding Dong! merrily on high
In heav'n the bells are ringing
Ding, dong! verily the sky
Is riv'n with angel singing
Gloria, Hosanna in excelsis.

The First Nowell

Source: English traditional

1. The first Nowell the Angel did say
Was to certain poor Shepherds in fields as they lay.
In fields where they lay keeping their sheep,
In a cold winter's night that was so deep.

Chorus
Nowell, nowell, nowell, nowell.
Born is the King of Israel.

From Heaven Above to Earth I Come

Words: Martin Luther, 1535; translated by Catherine
Winkworth, 1855

1. From heaven above to earth I come
To bear good news to every home;
Glad tidings of great joy I bring,
Whereof I now will say and sing.

Gloucestershire Wassail

Words and music: English traditional

1. Wassail! wassail! all over the town,
Our toast it is white and our ale it is brown;
Our bowl it is made of the white maple tree;
With the wassailing bowl, we'll drink to thee.

Go Tell It on the Mountain

John Wesley Work Jr., 1907; based on an African American
Spiritual, early 1800s

1. While shepherds kept their watching
O'er silent flocks by night,
Behold throughout the heavens
There shone a holy light

Chorus
Go, tell it on the mountain
Over the hills and everywhere
Go, tell it on the mountain
That Jesus Christ is born.

God Rest Ye Merry, Gentlemen

Source: English traditional

1. God rest ye merry, gentlemen,
Let nothing you dismay.
For Jesus Christ our Savior,
Was born on Christmas Day;
To save us all from Satan's power,
When we were gone astray.

Chorus
O tidings of comfort and joy,
For Jesus Christ our Savior
Was born on Christmas day.

Good Christian Men, Rejoice

Words: attributed to Heinrich Suso (1295–1366); translated
by John Mason Neale

1. Good Christian men, rejoice
With heart, and soul, and voice;
Give ye heed to what we say:
News! News!
Jesus Christ was born to-day:
Ox and ass before Him bow,
And He is in the manger now.
Christ is born today! Christ is born today.

Good King Wenceslas

Words: John Mason Neale (1818–1866)

1. Good King Wenceslas look'd out,
On the Feast of Stephen;
When the snow lay round about,
Deep, and crisp, and even:
Brightly shone the moon that night,
Though the frost was cruel,
When a poor man came in sight,
Gath'ring winter fuel.

Hallelujah Chorus

Words and music: from *The Messiah*, George Frideric Handel
(1685–1759)

Halleluiah!
For the Lord God Omnipotent reigneth.
The kingdom of this world
is become the Kingdom of our Lord,
and of His Christ,
and He shall reign forever and ever.
King of Kings, and Lord of Lords,
and He shall reign forever and ever.
Halleluiah!

Hark! The Herald Angels Sing

Words: Charles Wesley (1707–1788); amended by George
Whitefield (1714–1770)

1. Hark! The Herald Angels sing,
"Glory to the new-born King;
Peace on earth, and mercy mild,
God and sinners reconciled!"
Joyful, all ye nations, rise.
Join the triumph of the skies.
With th' Angelic Hosts proclaim,
"Christ is born in Bethlehem!"
Hark! the herald angels sing,
"Glory to the new-born King."

Here We Come A Wassailing

Words: English traditional

1. Here we come a wassailing
Among the leaves so green,
Here we come a wandering
So fair to be seen.

Chorus
Love and joy come to you,
And to you your wassail too,
And God bless you and send you a happy New Year.
And God send you a happy New Year.

225

The Holly and the Ivy

Words: traditional

1. The holly and the ivy,
Now both are full well grown.
Of all the trees that are in the wood,
The holly bears the crown.

Chorus
Oh, the rising of the sun,
The running of the deer.
The playing of the merry organ,
Sweet singing in the quire.

The Huron Carol

Words: St. Jean de Brébeuf (1593–1649); translated by Jesse
Edgar Middleton, 1926

1. 'Twas in the moon of winter-time
When all the birds had fled,
That mighty Gitchi Manitou
Sent angel choirs instead;
Before their light the stars grew dim,
And wandering hunter heard the hymn:

Refrain:
"Jesus your King is born, Jesus is born,
In excelsis gloria."

I Heard the Bells on Christmas Day

Words: Henry Wadsworth Longfellow, 1864

1. I heard the bells on Christmas day
Their old familiar carols play,
And wild and sweet the words repeat
Of peace on earth, good will to men.

I Saw Three Ships

Words: English traditional

1. I saw three ships come sailing in,
On Christmas day, on Christmas day,
I saw three ships come sailing in,
On Christmas day in the morning.

I Wonder as I Wander

Words and music: Appalachian carol; collected by John Jacob
Niles (1892–1980)

1. I wonder as I wander out under the sky,
How Jesus the Savior did come for to die.
For poor on'ry people like you and like I...
I wonder as I wander out under the sky.

In the Bleak Midwinter

Words: Christina Georgina Rossetti (1830–1894)

1. In the bleak mid-winter
Frosty wind made moan,
Earth stood hard as iron,
Water like a stone;
Snow had fallen, snow on snow,
Snow on snow,
In the bleak mid-winter
Long ago.

It Came Upon the Midnight Clear

Words: Edmund Hamilton Sears (1810–1876)

1. It came upon the midnight clear,
That glorious song of old,
From angels bending near the earth
To touch their harps of gold;
"Peace on the earth, good will to men
From heaven's all-gracious King"—
The world in solemn stillness lay
To hear the angels sing.

Jingle Bells

Words and music: James Pierpont (1822–1893)

1. Dashing thro' the snow,
In a one horse open sleigh,
O'er the hills we go,
Laughing all the way;
Bells on bob tail ring,
Making spirits bright,
Oh what sport to ride and sing
A sleighing song to night.

Chorus:
Jingle bells, Jingle bells,
Jingle all the way;
Oh! what joy it is to ride
In a one horse open sleigh.
Jingle bells, Jingle bells,
Jingle all the way
Oh! what joy it is to ride
In a one horse open sleigh.

Joy to the World

Words: Isaac Watts (1674–1748)

1. Joy to the world! The Lord is come:
Let earth receive her King,
Let every heart prepare him room,
And heaven and nature sing.

Miss Fogarty's Christmas Cake

Words and music: C. Frank Horn, 1883

1. As I sat in my window last evening,
The letterman brought it to me
A little gilt-edged invitation sayin'
"Gilhooley come over to tea"
I knew that the Fogarties sent it.
So I went just for old friendships sake.
The first thing they gave me to tackle
Was a slice of Miss Fogarty's cake.

Chorus:
There were plums and prunes and cherries,
There were citrons and raisins and cinnamon, too
There was nutmeg, cloves and berries
And a crust that was nailed on with glue
There were caraway seeds in abundance
Such that work up a fine stomach ache
That could kill a man twice after eating a slice
Of Miss Fogarty's Christmas cake.

O Come, All Ye Faithful

Words: "Adeste Fideles"; translated by Frederick Oakeley
(1802–1880)

1. O come, all ye faithful, joyful and triumphant,
O Come ye, O come ye, to Bethlehem.
Come and behold Him, born the King of Angels;

Chorus
O come, let us adore Him,
O come, let us adore Him,
O come, let us adore Him, Christ the Lord.

O Come, O Come, Emmanuel

Words: authorship unknown, 8th-century Latin; translated by
John Mason Neale

1. O come, O come, Emmanuel,
And ransom captive Israel,
That mourns in lonely exile here
Until the Son of God appear.

Refrain
Rejoice! Rejoice! Emmanuel
Shall come to thee, O Israel.

O Holy Night

Words: Placide Cappeau (1808–1877); translated by John Sullivan Dwight (1813–1893)

1. O holy night, the stars are brightly shining,
It is the night of the dear Savior's birth;
Long lay the world in sin and error pining,
Till He appeared and the soul felt its worth.
A thrill of hope the weary world rejoices,
For yonder breaks a new and glorious morn;

Chorus
Fall on your knees, Oh hear the angel voices!
O night divine, O night when Christ was born!
O night, O holy night, O night divine.

O Little Town of Bethlehem

Words: Phillips Brooks (1835–1893)

1. O little town of Bethlehem,
How still we see thee lie!
Above thy deep and dreamless sleep
The silent stars go by.
Yet in thy dark streets shineth
The everlasting Light;
The hopes and fears of all the years
Are met in thee to-night.

Once in Royal David's City

Words: Cecil Frances Alexander (1818–1895)

1. Once in royal David's city
Stood a lowly cattle shed,
Where a mother laid her Baby
In a manger for His bed:
Mary was that mother mild,
Jesus Christ her little Child.

The Seven Joys of Mary

Words and music: English traditional

1. The very first joy that Mary had,
It was the joy of one
To see her blessed Jesus
When He was first her Son
When He was first her Son.

Chorus
When He was Her first Son, Good Lord;
And happy may we be,
Praise Father, Son, and Holy Ghost
To all eternity

Silent Night, Holy Night

Words: Joseph Mohr (1792–1848); translated by John
Freeman Young (1820–1885)

1. Silent night! Holy night!
All is calm, all is bright,
Round yon Virgin Mother and Child!
Holy Infant, so tender and mild,
Sleep in heavenly peace!
Sleep in heavenly peace!

The Sussex Carol

Words and music collected by Ralph Vaughan Williams
(1872–1958)

1. On Christmas night true Christians sing
To hear what news the angel bring
News of great joy, cause of great mirth
Good tidings of the Savior's birth
Good tidings of the Savior's birth

The Twelve Days of Christmas

Words and music: English traditional

On the first day of Christmas,
My true love sent to me
A partridge in a pear tree.

On the second day of Christmas,
My true love sent to me
Two turtle-doves and
A partridge in a pear tree.

On the third day of Christmas,
My true love sent to me
Three French hens…

Up on the Housetop

Words and music: Benjamin Hanby (1833–1867)

1. Up on the housetop reindeer pause,
Out jumps good old Santa Claus.
Down through the chimney with lots of toys,
All for the little ones, Christmas joys.

Chorus
Ho, ho, ho! Who wouldn't go.
Ho, ho, ho! Who wouldn't go!
Up on the housetop, click, click, click.
Down through the chimney with good Saint Nick.

We Three Kings

Words and music: John Henry Hopkins Jr. (1820–1891)

1. We three kings of Orient are
Bearing gifts, we traverse afar.
Field and fountain, moor and mountain,
Following yonder star.

Chorus
O Star of Wonder, Star of Night,
Star with Royal Beauty bright,
Westward leading, Still proceeding,
Guide us to Thy perfect Light.

We Wish You a Merry Christmas

Words: English traditional

1. We wish you a merry Christmas,
We wish you a merry Christmas,
We wish you a merry Christmas and a Happy New Year!

Refrain
Good tidings we bring for you and your kin;
We wish you a merry Christmas and a Happy New Year!

The Wexford Carol

Words and music: unknown

1. Good people all, this Christmas-time,
Consider well and bear in mind
What our good God for us has done
In sending his beloved Son.
With Mary holy we should pray
To God with love this Christmas day;
In Bethlehem upon that morn
There was a blessed Messiah born.

What Child Is This?

Words: William Chatterton Dix (1837–1898)

1. What Child is this who, laid to rest
On Mary's lap is sleeping?
Whom Angels greet with anthems sweet,
While shepherds watch are keeping?

This, this is Christ the King,
Whom shepherds guard and Angels sing;
Haste, haste, to bring Him laud,
The Babe, the Son of Mary.

While Shepherds Watched Their Flocks by Night

Words: Nahum Tate (1652–1715)

1. While Shepherds watched their flocks by night,
All seated on the ground,
The Angel of the Lord came down,
And glory shone all around.

The Worcestershire Carol

Words and music: William Henry Havergal (1793–1870)

1. How grand and how bright
That wonderful night,
When angels to Bethlehem came!
They burst forth like fires,
They struck their gold lyres,
And mingled their song with the flame.

ABOUT THE ILLUSTRATORS

Roger Garcia

Roger Garcia lived in El Salvador until he was seven years old, when his parents moved him to North America. Because of the language barrier, he had to find a way to communicate with other kids. That's when he discovered the art of tracing. It wasn't long before he mastered this highly skilled technique, and by age 14, he was drawing cartoons for a weekly newspaper. He taught himself to paint and sculpt, and then in high school and college, Roger skipped class to hide in the art room all day in order to further explore his talent.

Peter Tyler

Peter is a recent graduate of the Vancouver Film School Visual Art and Design, and Classical animation programs. Though his ultimate passion is filmmaking, he is also intent on developing his draftsmanship and storytelling, with the aim of using those skills in future filmic misadventures.

Roly Wood

Roly has worked in Toronto as a freelance illustrator, and was also employed in the graphic design department of a landscape architecture firm. In 2004 he wrote and illustrated a historical comic book set in Lang Pioneer Village near Peterborough, Ontario. To see more of Roly's work, visit www.rolywood.com.

Patrick Hénaff

Born in France, Patrick Hénaff is mostly self-taught. He is a versatile artist who has explored a variety of media under many different influences. He now uses primarily pen and ink to draw and then processes the images on computer. He is particularly interested in the narrative power of pictures and tries to use them as a way to tell stories.

ABOUT THE AUTHOR

Courtesy: Amy Lambert

Tonya Lambert is an author and historian who currently resides in Edmonton, Alberta. She holds an MA in history from the University of Saskatchewan. Tonya has done a great deal of academic writing and has worked in the publishing sector as an indexer, transcriber, editor and bookseller, but her real love is writing. In recent years she has taken a keen interest in popular culture, specifically holiday themes. An earlier work, *Halloween Trivia*, was published by Blue Bike Books. Tonya is also the single mother of three girls, who keep her constantly on the go.

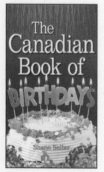